# Notes on the Preparation of Essays in the Arts and Sciences

Fourth Edition, revised and expanded

Fourth Edition Revised and Edited by
Lucille Strath
Heather Avery
Karen Taylor

Academic Skills Centre
Trent University
Peterborough, Ontario
Canada, K9J 7B8

1993

# Notes on the Preparation of Essays in the Arts and Sciences

Printed by Webcom in Canada
Fourth Edition

Canadian Cataloguing in Publication Data

Main entry under title

Notes on the preparation of essays in the arts and sciences

4th ed., rev. and expanded.
Revised and edited by Lucille Strath, Heather Avery, Karen Taylor


1. Report writing.    2. English language—Rhetoric.
I. Strath, Lucille    II. Avery, Heather    III. Taylor, Karen   (Karen E.)
IV. Trent University.    Academic Skills Centre.

LB2369.N68 1993        808'.042        C93-094082-2

ISBN 0-9693668-5-X

Published by the Academic Skills Centre, Trent University,
Peterborough, Ontario, Canada, K9J 7B8

# Dedication

This book is dedicated to the writers of its earlier editions without whose vision and persistence this present text could not have been written:

Peter Slade
Annette Tromly
Richard Harrison
Isabel Henniger
Sheree-Lee Powsey
Kari Lie
Linda Zernask

# Contents

# Preface

With the release of this fourth edition of *Notes on the Preparation of Essays in the Arts and Sciences,* we celebrate the twenty-eight years it has been in existence. What began in the mid-1960s as a slim booklet designed to assist undergraduate English students at Trent University has now become a substantial guide to methods of documentation in the arts and sciences. Over the years, thousands of copies have assisted students with the formal requirements of academic writing. By the 1980s, copies of *Notes* were being distributed across Canada and, through the International Baccalaureate Schools, around the world. Today, this small guide is a national best-seller.

Although this new edition contains many of the features of previous editions, revisions have been made throughout in an attempt to make the documentation methods easier to locate and the information concerning each method more complete. Our coverage of APA style (here set out as parenthetical documentation Style B) and the CBE number-reference method has been expanded to assist students writing in the social and natural sciences; Part V, "Documentation Methods by Academic Discipline," has been expanded to include most of the documentation information students need to know when writing papers in a wide variety of disciplines. Every effort was made to make certain that all the standard documentation methods that an undergraduate student might require are contained in this one book.

The sections on punctuation, grammar, and correction symbols have been deleted because they are dealt with fully in the Academic Skills Centre's *Clear, Correct, Creative: A Handbook for Writers of Academic Prose.* Even though the essay writing process is covered in the second edition of *Thinking It Through: A Practical Guide to Academic Essay Writing*, we have revised and retained Part 1 on writing the essay because many students and teachers have written to tell us that this section provided them with a clear and succinct introduction to the requirements of the academic essay. As well, the chapter reminds students that form serves substance: an essay can be formally correct and still be without value in content and meaning.

Acknowledging and referencing sources of information are two of the main distinguishing features of all academic writing. They demand completeness, accuracy, and consistency in both form and style. However, we would like to remind students using this book that once the proper forms and styles are learned and adhered to, writers are free to find their own voice, free to get on with the even more important task of expressing their thoughts and reporting their findings.

June 1993
Peterborough, Ontario
Canada

# Acknowledgements

Writers of guide books such as this one are gatherers and sorters—we belong to a vast company of stylists who work to achieve rational standards of form. Variations—an upstart colon here, an unexpected double-space there—are greeted with the same alarm as the wearer of a bathing suit would be in a boardroom. We chase down the variant until we are satisfied that it has the credentials of proper form. The present writers are indebted to all those gatherers and sorters who have gone before us, those who have set down the documentation methods we have described here. We thank particularly those writers of the previous editions, to whom this book is dedicated.

Special thanks are due also to our colleagues Maged el Komos and Martin Boyne, who read the manuscript and offered valuable suggestions. As well, our thanks go to Patricia Doyon, who kept our office running smoothly while we were occupied in periods of writing and editing. And, as in many of our past publishing projects, we are especially grateful to Barbara Fox for preparing this manuscript for printing.

# _____ PART I: PREPARATION _____

Writing a university essay is a particular kind of learning, an experience students may or may not have encountered in their earlier education. What may be new to students is the expectation that the essay should be, above all, an exercise in thinking. The essay is not meant to include everything a student knows about a topic nor to catalogue pages of unassimilated information. Rather, its purpose is to examine and interpret a body of material. In addition to describing a subject, such as an historical event or a repeated image in a poem, the essay will usually examine the why and how of the subject. In an essay, the material is analyzed; the writer finds a means by which to account for the evidence examined and in doing so makes this evidence coherent and logical. An essay may, for instance, isolate a cause of an historical event, or it may explain the function of a poetic image. In short, the essay gives students a chance to show, not merely that they have acquired information, but that they can reflect upon and learn from this information and use it to advance or defend a claim.

As the next few pages indicate, essay writing involves a number of stages, stages which are treated here as separate and distinct steps in a process. It is important to remember, though, that the process is never simple, and that it is always fluid; the stages merge and separate, expand and contract, depending upon the nature of the material being treated. Even the most methodical writers will change their procedures somewhat with every essay. And many writers depart from set patterns as they become more experienced at writing essays and as they develop their own styles. The scheme described here for the preparation of essays is meant to be a flexible guideline, not a prescriptive set of rules. For those students who are either learning essay-writing skills for the first time or faced with especially stubborn materials, the method will offer direction and, we hope, encouragement.

## PLANNING THE ESSAY

### From Topic to Thesis

Essay assignments come in many different forms. Sometimes—especially in upper-year courses—the topic is left entirely to the student. Sometimes an instructor designates a broad subject area which the student will need to narrow to a manageable size. And sometimes a more focused essay topic is assigned—perhaps in the form of a question, a problem to solve, a statement to evaluate, or a quotation to discuss. Regardless of the form your topic takes, the process of writing an essay involves moving from a general understanding of a topic to a clear presentation of a perspective on that topic. The process begins as a question; even if your topic does not ask a question, you should decide on a query that you want your essay to investigate. The process ends in what, to the best of your knowledge and abilities, you decide is an answer to that question. In writing an essay, then, you will be making clear your answer. But the essay is never the final word. It is written to say, "This is the conclusion to which my thinking and reading to date have brought me."

Once you have been assigned—or have chosen—a topic, begin your essay by thinking about that topic. Look to your reading on the subject, your ideas, your lectures, and your conversations with others. Your goal should be to discover a central question or a problem, the first step in the development of a THESIS, or controlling idea. This thesis is the answer to your central question, or a solution to your central problem, indicating both what the essay will address and how your analysis will proceed.

The exact time at which you develop your thesis will vary from essay to essay. You should be thinking toward a thesis even in the earliest stages of research. Of course, you cannot arrive at a final thesis until you have completed your research—you do not know the answer yet!—but giving some thought to a controlling idea at an early stage will help you direct your research efforts.

Moreover, an appropriate thesis is key to a good essay. Keep in mind that the thesis of your essay should never be self-evident: "Charles Darwin is associated with evolution" is not a thesis. The thesis is a position or perspective, defended or explained by a carefully planned structure of ideas supported by evidence. It can be, but is not necessarily, controversial. "Charles Darwin's ideas are outrageous" and "Charles Darwin's Origin of Species was the first coherent expression of the theory of evolution" are both theses, though the former is a more argumentative (in the colloquial sense of the word) statement.

Remember that the thesis of an essay is different from its topic; it goes beyond the topic to make an assertion. Usually you will assert your controlling idea in what is called the THESIS STATEMENT. If your topic, for example, is "Charles Darwin's contribution to knowledge," your thesis statement will make some sort of assertion about that topic. Figure I (p. 9) shows the outline of an essay written on this topic with the following thesis statement: "Charles Darwin did not invent the theory of evolution. However, backed by careful observation, Origin of Species presented such a coherent expression of the theory that the burden of proof shifted from the supporters of evolution to those who denied its validity." The thesis statement, then, states what the essay is claiming and the method by which that claim will be explained and supported. It expresses, in a general but precise statement, the analytic purpose of the essay. It focuses your essay, and coordinates and synthesizes your thinking, research, and writing. Most often, the thesis statement will be brief—no more than a sentence or two. Usually, it will appear in a prominent place in your essay: often in the introductory paragraphs, but sometimes not until the conclusion.

Though it is best to try to express your thesis in a single statement, if this seems impossible, do not be alarmed. Some essays do not lend themselves to such a compressed treatment of their main claim. A thesis which unfolds more gradually—perhaps through several separate points made throughout the essay—can also be effective. But remember that there must be no doubt in the mind of either writer or reader about just what constitutes the essay's central assertion. And you must know your thesis before you start to write the final draft of your essay.

For many students, finding a thesis is the most difficult part of writing an essay. When you are having trouble coming up with a central idea, try making a planning sheet; list all the important and interesting ideas that have occurred to you about the topic in your reading and thinking, and see if you can find one that you want to emphasize or develop, or several that you want to relate in some way. If you are still undecided about a thesis, try discussing your ideas with a friend or classmate, or doing some exploratory writing. Often just expressing your thoughts, either out loud or on paper, can help you discover a controlling idea with which you can begin work.

### The Writer's Involvement

Students often ask to what extent "their own ideas" should be part of their essays. Students' ideas are always part of their essays. First, each writer brings his or her own ideas to the essay in choosing how to analyze and how to describe the subject being treated. Admittedly, certain essays will leave less room than others for the student to invent methods for explaining the subject matter or even to choose among established methods. However, all composition involves this individual process of selecting and ordering material.

Second, in the sense in which "their own ideas" means "their own interpretations," students can—and should be prepared to—contribute their own thoughts on their material. However, contributing your own thought does not mean that you should include unargued or unsupported assertions based solely on the sincerity of your own belief in them. Be prepared to discuss what you believe in your essays, but be prepared also to hold your own ideas up to the same critical light under which you look at the ideas of others.

## RESEARCHING THE ESSAY

Not all essays require consulting dozens of books and articles. In an English course, for example, you may be asked to use only a play or a poem as your research material; your observations on the work and the argument you extract from these observations will constitute your entire essay. But all essays you write will require some form of research, of collecting information, in either primary or secondary sources or both.[1] It is important to undertake the essay with a clear idea of how one goes about collecting this information.

Some students think of research as a fairly passive process that goes on prior to—and apart from—the planning of an essay. These students are likely to spend many wasted hours in the library, taking notes on a very broad (and sometimes vaguely defined) topic. They put off doing any directed thinking about the claims and structure of their essay until after their notes have accumulated. The more efficient way to work is to be planning and doing research <u>at the same time</u>. Research is more than mere notetaking: it involves getting an overview of your topic, narrowing the topic, selecting the most useful sources, thinking toward a thesis, and, finally, collecting information directed to a particular end.

---

[1]For an explanation of primary and secondary sources, see pages 32 and 33 of Part III.

## Selecting Material

Once you have chosen a topic and rephrased it as a question or a tentative assertion, research should begin—and you must work actively. From the minute that you open a book, you are working not only to collect information but also to plan the essay and further define an appropriate thesis. Moreover, you also want to discover a way of considering your topic that permits you to write a paper of appropriate length in the time you have allotted. As you work, write. It is probably not advisable to take content notes as soon as you open a book, but it certainly is worthwhile to jot down ideas that strike you, to play at rewording your thesis, to sketch tentative outlines, even to draft a few paragraphs when a particular aspect of your paper becomes clear.

Researching usually proceeds most smoothly if you work to gain a general understanding of your topic before reading in detail about specifics. If you are using secondary sources, quickly reading or skimming one or two short but general works on your topic (books, articles, even encyclopaedia articles) and looking at the tables of contents in other books on the subject will help you see what questions or controlling ideas might be fruitful.

Another useful step is to compile a working bibliography (a list of potentially useful books and articles). The Library of Congress Subject Headings, the card catalogue, bibliographies, indexes, and abstracts will help you; the reference librarian will show you how to use these tools. Gather a wide selection of texts for your working bibliography; remember, at this stage your final thesis is still undetermined, so it will be difficult to know exactly which works will ultimately be most useful to you. Once you have a working bibliography, check the table of contents and the index of each book to see how each work relates to your topic; skim the introductory and summary chapters (or the introductory and summary paragraphs of articles), as well as the relevant sections of the text, to determine what the argument of each work is and to see how these various perspectives might affect your own thesis.

As you skim, you must evaluate. The date of publication will sometimes aid you in assessing the importance of a text. In some disciplines (for example, the sciences) you will need information that is up-to-date. In other disciplines you may not want the most recent works; in history, for instance, works contemporary with your subject may be particularly useful. Noting who wrote the book or article might help also. (Is the author well respected in the field? Do you recognize any biases?) Do not, however, aim simply to choose works which support one another; an essay that tries to come to terms with evidence that is contradictory or opinions that conflict will be superior to one that ignores problem areas.

At this stage, you probably will not want to read carefully or take content notes—you are simply deciding what must be read. However, you may still want to write: to jot down responses to new information, to record insights, to make note of key details. Chances are, the more you interact with the material, by talking about it or writing about it, the better you will understand it when the time comes to draft the paper.

## Taking Notes

Once you have a rough idea of the material you need to read and can formulate a tentative thesis (and perhaps can recognize what the sections of your paper might be), you are ready to take content notes. This thesis and outline can be revised and developed as you read, take notes, and write, but having them roughed out at this stage will give direction to your notetaking. Remember, the aim is not to gather a great mass of notes but to gather notes directed to a particular end. Keeping in mind the approximate length of each section of your paper will help you keep your notes brief and to the point; making decisions now about what is important enough to use, and therefore to note, will make the actual writing much easier.

At this stage, you should prepare bibliographic note cards for every source consulted. There are certain standard pieces of information you will need to complete any citation: author, title, and publication information. Consult the recommended documentation style for your discipline and see what information you will need to provide about each source. Completing a bibliographic card before taking content notes will ensure that you do not have to return to the library the day your essay is due to complete a list of works cited.

When you finally come to take content notes, do not read books and articles slavishly from beginning to end. Read with a purpose—to find particular kinds of information. Furthermore, read critically. Distinguish between fact and opinion, and when a writer puts a certain interpretation on a piece of evidence, ask yourself whether that is the only interpretation possible and whether other evidence supports the argument.

As for the notes themselves, they can take a variety of forms. Most of your notes will probably paraphrase information contained in a source: reformulating material in your own words at this point will improve your understanding and will make the writing of the essay easier. You may also choose to copy short passages directly, particularly from primary sources. Statistics, you may simply record. Be careful in your notes, however, to distinguish between quoted and paraphrased material. It will be important when you write your essay to know what material merely needs a citation and what material must be treated as a direct quotation.

You may make your notes either on file cards or on ordinary paper. Be sure to record page numbers and any other pertinent documentation not recorded on your bibliographic cards. If you use file cards, put only one fact or idea on each card. Later, when your outline is fully developed, you will be able to label each note to indicate where it belongs in the outline and to put the cards in the order in which the points should appear in the essay. If you make your notes on paper, leave wide margins so that you can add your own comments or cross-refer to other notes. Taking notes on only one side of the page will permit cutting and pasting.

## ORGANIZING THE ESSAY

Once you have established your thesis and have some grasp of your research material, you can concentrate on organization to make sure that all the sections will work together to demonstrate your main idea. An OUTLINE provides a good opportunity for exploring how the essay will be organized, and the best kind of outline is that which helps you develop your thesis. Often you will find that the thesis statement suggests its own organizing principles: the main steps by which you establish your argument or demonstrate your thesis will become the main sections and subsections of your essay. Regardless of whether this is true, everything in your outline should be, implicitly or explicitly, relevant to the central assertion you have chosen. This is why single-word headings in outlines are not useful; you need instead to use statements that focus your thought. In this way, the outline will allow you to refine your thinking about your argument. When you see your argument as a physical picture on a page, you will be able to determine more easily what should be emphasized, what should be of greater, equal, or subordinate importance, what should be deleted, what should be expanded, and what should be rearranged.

As you draw your outline, pay careful attention to the structure of assertions and evidence in your plan. Remember that you are trying to show your reader the validity of something (your thesis or main assertion) through the careful use of supporting material (your evidence). Figure I shows an outline for an essay with a fairly complicated thesis. Like the thesis in this example, your thesis statement should be adequately developed through several "sub-theses"—assertions into which you have divided your controlling idea for analysis. Attached to each sub-thesis will be evidence relevant to that particular idea. This evidence, in turn, may be further subdivided. As the evidence backs up each sub-thesis and each sub-thesis backs up the thesis, a strong and cohesive demonstration of your thinking will be presented.

During the writing stage, almost everyone discovers new things to say, new ideas, or new arrangements of ideas. If you have at least a basis from which to work, and to which you can return if the new ideas do not turn out to be helpful, you can more readily explore lines of argument. Not having an outline, on the other hand, either through not giving yourself time to organize your ideas properly or through neglecting to make a plan, means that you are writing the essay "out of your head" and may only be unpacking the contents of your mind onto the page in an unorganized way.

Sometimes and for some writers, however, preparing an outline in advance of drafting is very difficult. When this is the case, a very quick rough draft may be the best way to begin writing. From the rough draft, an outline should emerge, and from it the writer can prepare a second, more organized, version of the essay.

## FIGURE I: A SAMPLE OUTLINE

| | |
|---|---|
| THESIS | Charles Darwin did not invent the theory of evolution. However, backed by careful observation, Origin of Species presented such a coherent expression of the theory that the burden of proof shifted from the supporters of evolution to those who denied it. |

First Sub-thesis    I.    Evolutionary theory was not new; it was
before Darwin, part of the history of biology.

first supporting point    A.   There were other evolutionary theorists.
evidence                     1.  Aristotle
                               2.  Erasmus Darwin

second supporting point    B.   Darwin's debt to these thinkers
evidence                     1.  Darwin's own acknowledgement
                               2.  Huxley on Darwin

Second Sub-thesis    II.   Darwin's observations were thorough. They made
the notions of adaptation and selection plausible.

first supporting point    A.   The relationship between structure and function
in finches' beaks

second supporting point    B.   How selective breeding produced "better"
domestic animals

Third Sub-thesis    III.  If those who wrote after Origin of Species wanted
to deny evolution, they had to develop better
explanations for evidence they all acknowledged.

evidence    A.   Religious opponents
evidence    B.   Scientific opponents

# WRITING THE ESSAY

At one time or another, almost all students suffer from writer's block; staring at a blank sheet or screen before you begin to write a draft can be a frightening experience. If you have spent some time carefully researching and planning the essay, however, you are less likely to stall at the beginning. Yet even a well-planned essay can be difficult to begin. If it is, the main thing to do is to start writing. Once you have broken through your initial resistance and have begun to fill the blank space in front of you, ideas will begin to flow. Your first draft, after all, is not what you will submit; consider it as a rough effort—something you will be able to revise later—and the void may seem less forbidding.

## The First Draft

The stages in the preparation of an essay are never completely separate; the most carefully planned essay will always require further thinking during the writing stage. Indeed, in the act of writing you will often discover ideas or clarify thoughts; you can write to find out what you think. Once you have established a basic plan, it is useful to sketch a rough draft fairly quickly, while the ideas are still fresh. At the earliest stages of writing, exact expression is less important than overall shaping. Concentrate first on getting your ideas down on paper; allow time for revision later.

Many people find that the INTRODUCTION and the CONCLUSION are the most difficult parts of the essay to write. Remember that you need not begin your rough draft at the beginning; often introductions can be more effectively written after other sections of the draft have been completed. Instead of trying to compose a graceful and eloquent introduction immediately, just write down your thesis and then start to develop the first sub-thesis in your outline.

When you do compose the introduction, keep the following in mind. In general, the beginning of an essay has two purposes: to capture the reader's interest and to introduce your material. Avoid beginnings which are too general, too theoretical, or too far removed from the essay's central concerns. When concluding, you should manage to avoid two extremes. On the one hand, do not write a conclusion which restates your argument in exactly the same words you have used throughout the essay; such repetition provides only a mechanical ending, which will not be interesting to your reader. (It is important, though, to remind your reader of your thesis in the conclusion.) On the other hand, be careful not to introduce entirely new ideas in your final paragraph; your reader will be frustrated if the essay suddenly presents unresolved issues. One useful compromise between these two extremes might be to widen the perspective on your subject somewhat by suggesting how it has implications beyond the ones with which you have dealt.

## Revising and Proofreading

After you have written your essay in a rough form, pay close attention to revising the draft. Adopt a method for revising systematically. One useful scheme is to read the draft several times, paying attention to one aspect of the essay (content, organization, use of language, mechanics) at a time.

It is probably best to pay attention to organization first. Your task at this level of revision is to create a structure that will help your reader see how all aspects of the paper relate to your main thesis. Using your outline as a guide, check your draft to ensure that you have composed sentences which articulate the sub-thesis of each section and its relation to the main thesis. Then, ensure that in the paragraphs of each section the relationship of each paragraph to the sub-thesis is clear. Remember that ideas relate in very precise ways; one part of your essay can exemplify, contradict, expand, or qualify another. Linking words (such as "however," "nevertheless," "therefore," "conversely") can help you clarify for your reader the logical connections between thoughts.

Within paragraphs, use transitional devices such as linking words, repetition of key terms, and pronouns so that the reader can see easily how an idea is being developed. Keep in mind that a paragraph shorter than three sentences generally does not develop an idea fully and that a paragraph longer than a double-spaced typewritten page (300 words) may be difficult for a reader to follow.

Even the smallest unit in your essay—the individual word—will require careful thought at some stage of revision. Subtle differences in meaning can make one word considerably more appropriate than another. Have a good dictionary and a thesaurus on your desk; both of these tools can help you distinguish words from one another and find alternative and more precise ways to express your thoughts. Be aware also of the difference between denotations (dictionary meanings) and connotations (meanings acquired through use). The dictionary might define green as a colour, but this word has also come to be associated connotatively with environmental protection. Finally, remember that the context in which a word is used can affect its appropriateness. The word "interface," for instance, has a precise meaning in the field of computer science, but in other disciplines it might be no more than vague and empty jargon. During the final stages of revision, pay careful attention to matters of expression.

Have you in every case chosen the clearest phrasing, the most appropriate language, and the most precise words to convey your ideas?

Proofreading—the final stage of essay preparation—should not be forgotten. It is worse to hand in a sloppily typed, uncorrected essay than a neat handwritten one. Putting the best face on your essay, by submitting a clear copy with ample margins and careful spelling, is certain to make a difference. Many mistakes in writing, typing, grammar, or spelling can be picked up by <u>reading your draft aloud</u> at least once. In the final stage of preparation, the title page and documentation sections will also need your attention. Choose a title that reflects fairly specifically what your essay is about; overly clever, vague, or cryptic titles will only confuse your reader. For rules of documentation see Part IV

**Style**

As you turn your attention to the style of your essay, remember that you have two responsibilities: one to your reader and one to your material. For your reader you must make your ideas as accessible as possible. Use language which is precise and direct—free from overly complicated diction and passive, vague expressions. Always choose the most straightforward means of expression. This is not to say, however, that you should write using only simple, short words and sentences. Thoughtful ideas and explanations may well require complex sentence structures and a good vocabulary. Your second responsibility, indeed, is to the material of your essay, and your style must do justice to its complexity. Choose words which express accurately and completely what you mean to say, constructions which establish what is emphatic or subordinate in your thinking, transitions which clarify exactly how one thought relates to another. If you find yourself writing vaguely, and revisions seem inadequate, check to see if your words, particularly words that are key to your essay, reflect clearly what you are trying to say. Focus on a problem word or passage and ask yourself what its meaning is. Search for words that more accurately express that meaning.

Language which is simple and precise is suitable for an essay in any academic discipline. Certain small stylistic practices, however, may be encouraged by some departments and discouraged by others. For instance, it was generally the practice in the past to use the third person ("the researcher" or "one") when making reference to oneself in a scientific paper. The reasoning behind this practice was that the writer should be separate or detached from the argument presented. It is still the case that in a scientific experiment the passive voice rather than the active voice is used. We write, "The solution was heated to 40 C," rather than "I heated the solution to 40 C." However, it is now more widely recognized that the conclusion that you are arguing in scientific papers is the result of your own thinking based on the evidence that you have gathered. Thus, the use of "I" is more widely accepted, in science, social science and humanities papers because it is recognized that the author's mind informs every word in the paper. You should, if you are in doubt about this practice, ask your instructor or consult a leading journal in your discipline.

As you encounter essay writing in a number of different courses, try to develop an awareness of particular demands. Different disciplines, materials, and intended audiences will force you to change your writing style slightly. With practice you will be able to adapt your individual style to changing expectations.

This brief introduction to essay writing may not answer all your questions. For more detailed instruction, you should consult <u>Thinking It Through: A Practical Guide to Academic Essay Writing</u> (full bibliographic details in Part VIII). This text deals with all aspects of composition, from finding a topic to conducting research to drafting, revising, and proofreading. For more information on stylistic and grammatical concerns, <u>Clear, Correct, Creative: A Handbook for Writers of Academic Prose</u> will be helpful. This text introduces the reader to grammatical conventions and gives counsel on such matters as avoiding wordiness, using appropriate diction, and writing coherent paragraphs.

# PART II: FORMAT

**Preliminaries**

1. Use white paper of standard size (8 1/2 x 11 inches).
2. Type or print the essay using a computer printer, if possible. For hand-written essays, write in a clear hand on lined paper.
3. Write, type, or print on one side of the paper only.
4. Double-space all essays, whether typed, printed, or hand-written, and leave margins of 1 or 1 1/2 inches at the top, bottom, and both sides of the page so that the marker has room to make comments.
5. Number all pages, except the first, with arabic numerals in the top right-hand corner. Do not use a period, bracket, or any other punctuation mark after the page number.
6. Your name, the date, the title of the essay, and the name and number of the course (e.g., English 100) must be clearly indicated on a separate title page.
7. Staple or clip pages together at the top left-hand corner. Submit essays unfolded.
8. Some disciplines (such as Anthropology) permit, or even encourage, the use of headings and subheadings to indicate sections of the essay. Check with your instructor.

**Spelling**

Consult a reputable Canadian, British, or American dictionary for acceptable spelling. Choose one system of spelling and use it consistently throughout the essay.

**Splitting Words**

Generally, splitting words looks clumsy and should be avoided. If it is necessary to split a word at the end of a line, do so only at the end of a syllable: mat-ter (not matt-er); be-lief (not bel-ief); writ-ing (not wri-ting). When in doubt consult a dictionary.

**Abbreviations**

Abbreviations and acronyms are most commonly used when documenting source material. Sometimes, however, they are used in the text of an essay or research paper. When deciding whether to use an abbreviation or acronym, consider the reader. If your reader will be more familiar with the abbreviation than with the complete form it represents, use the abbreviation. Some examples might be BBC, DNA, IQ, NATO, OPEC, REM, Rh, and UNESCO. If, on the other hand, there is the slightest possibility that your reader will be confused by the abbreviation, consider not using it. Would spelling the term out throughout the paper be a nuisance? If you decide that you do want to use an abbreviation, for reasons of economy, even though your reader might be puzzled by it, spell the term out completely the first time, following this with the abbreviation in parentheses: General Agreement on Tariffs and Trade (GATT). Whatever you decide, be consistent throughout the paper, and, should you use abbreviations, use conventional forms. Any good general dictionary will list conventional abbreviations. Following there is a list of the abbreviated forms of the provinces, territories, and states of Canada and the United States. These abbreviations should be used in documentation, not in the text of an essay.

### CANADA

| | | | |
|------|------------------|-----|----------------------|
| AB | Alberta | NT | Northwest Territories |
| BC | British Columbia | ON | Ontario |
| MB | Manitoba | PE | Prince Edward Island |
| NB | New Brunswick | PQ | Quebec |
| NF | Newfoundland | SK | Saskatchewan |
| NS | Nova Scotia | YT | Yukon Territories |

### UNITED STATES

| | | | |
|------|----------------------|-----|-----------------|
| AL | Alabama | MO | Missouri |
| AK | Alaska | MT | Montana |
| AS | American Samoa | NE | Nebraska |
| AZ | Arizona | NV | Nevada |
| AR | Arkansas | NH | New Hampshire |
| CA | California | NJ | New Jersey |
| CZ | Canal Zone | NM | New Mexico |
| CO | Colorado | NY | New York |
| CT | Connecticut | NC | North Carolina |
| DE | Delaware | ND | North Dakota |
| DC | District of Columbia | OH | Ohio |
| FL | Florida | OK | Oklahoma |
| GA | Georgia | OR | Oregon |
| GU | Guam | PA | Pennsylvania |
| HI | Hawaii | PR | Puerto Rico |
| ID | Idaho | RI | Rhode Island |

| | | | | |
|---|---|---|---|---|
| IL | Illinois | SC | South Carolina |
| IN | Indiana | SD | South Dakota |
| IA | Iowa | TN | Tennessee |
| KS | Kansas | TX | Texas |
| KY | Kentucky | UT | Utah |
| LA | Louisiana | VT | Vermont |
| ME | Maine | VA | Virginia |
| MD | Maryland | VI | Virgin Islands |
| MA | Massachusetts | WA | Washington |
| MI | Michigan | WV | West Virginia |
| MN | Minnesota | WI | Wisconsin |
| MS | Mississippi | WY | Wyoming |

## Capitalization

Most English speakers are familiar with basic capitalization rules: people's names are capitalized, as are the names of places and the letters beginning sentences. In academic writing, however, it is often useful to know a few of the more intricate rules governing capitalization.

### 1. Proper Nouns

All proper nouns, which are nouns that name specific persons, places, and things, are capitalized. Proper nouns include, but are not limited to, the following: names of people (and their titles) and places; names of government departments, political parties, and organizations; names of institutions; names of nationalities and languages; names of races and tribes; names of specific deities, religions, and members of religions; names of departments, degrees and courses; names of historical movements, periods, events, and official documents. Common nouns, which refer more generally to objects, places, or people, are not capitalized.

| *Proper Nouns* | *Common Nouns* |
|---|---|
| Uncle George | my uncle |
| Professor Whetung | a university professor |
| Sioux City | the city |
| Ministry of Transportation | a provincial ministry |
| the Minister of Health; Minister | a health minister; |
| of Health and Welfare Judy LaMarsh | Judy LaMarsh, |
| | the minister of health and |
| | welfare |

16

| | |
|---|---|
| the Prime Minister, Prime Minister | the acting prime minister, |
| Pierre Trudeau | the former prime minister |
| New Democratic Party | a socialist party |
| Pollution Probe | an environmental lobby group |
| England, an English garden | a formal garden |
| Mohawk, Indian, Afro-American | a native tribe, white, black |
| God, Catholicism, a Catholic priest | a god, a religioius person |
| Geography Department, Geography 101 | studying geography |
| Trent University | a small university |
| Master of Arts | a master's degree |
| the Enlightenment, World War II | the eighteenth century, a war |
| Bill 101 | federal legislation |

## 2. Names of Languages and Derivatives

Any word that is also a name, or derived from a name, of a language is always capitalized.

| | |
|---|---|
| Spanish class | math class |
| French Canadian | my history essay |
| a German major | a language major |

## 3. Compass Directions, Seasons, and Geographic Regions

These are not capitalized unless they are part of a name or designate a particular part of the world.

| | |
|---|---|
| North Bay; the Far North | north; the north of Canada |
| the South; South Carolina | south; a southern state |
| the Far East; the Eastern Townships | east; eastern Newfoundland |
| the West; the Western world | west; western Canadian grain |
| the Spring Gala | summer, spring |
| the Winter Festival | winter, fall |
| the Prairie provinces; the Prairies (Alberta, Sasktchewan, and Manitoba | a prairie; across the prairies |
| the Maritime provinces; the Maritimes (Nova Scotia, New Brunswick, and Prince Edward Island) | maritime regions |
| the Arctic; the Arctic Circle | arctic temperatures |

17

4. Adjectives derived from the names of legislative bodies are usually capitalized.

Senate reform
a House committee

5. The plural forms of words such as government, department, river, and state are not capitalized even when they designate specific bodies.

| | |
|---|---|
| the Department of Finance | the departments of Finance, Transportation, and Fisheries |
| the Kluane River | the Kluane and Mackenzie rivers |
| New York State | the New England states |

6. The title of an individual is capitalized only for a political or judicial office-holder, not for an officer in the private sector or in an organization or appointed government body.

| | |
|---|---|
| Judge Granby | council chairman David Cooke |
| Premier Wells | company president Jacquie Doyon |

7. Periods of time are often capitalized when the reference is to a specific historical era with an historical label whose words could also be understood in a general sense; otherwise they are usually in lower case. When in doubt, follow the capitalization used in the majority of your sources.

| | |
|---|---|
| the Age of Reason | age of reason |
| the Middle Ages | antiquity |
| the Renaissance | the renaissance of art |
| the Reformation | the baroque period |
| the Enlightenment | this enlightened era |
| the Dirty Thirties | the thirties (the 1930s) |
| the Gay Nineties | the nineties (the 1990s) |
| the troubled Sixties | the sixties (the 1960s) |

8. Nouns and adjectives designating religious, philosophical, literary, artistic, and musical movements and styles are capitalized when they are derivatives of proper names or when it is necessary to distinguish the name of a style or movement from the same words used in a general sense. Otherwise, use lower-case letters.

| | |
|---|---|
| the Bauhaus | classical |
| Cartesian | cubism |
| Gothic | dadaism |
| the Group of Seven | existentialism |
| Methodism | humanism |
| the New Criticism | impressionism |
| Romanesque | realism |
| Victorian | romanticism |
| | structuralism |

9. Titles

In the text of your essay, the first and last words of a title are always capitalized as are all other major words of a title. Coordinating conjunctions, articles and short prepositions are not considered major words and are not capitalized. Always capitalize a word following a colon in a title, even if it is a coordinating conjunction, article or preposition. For titles of works in other languages, follow the conventions of the particular language.

*Book Titles*
History of Psychology
A Tale of Two Cities
The World of the Short Story
John Milton: Complete Poems
and Major Prose
The Oxford Companion to Canadian
History and Literature
Poets Between the Wars

*Article Titles*
"Private Lives, Public Virtues"
"How to Have an Extraordinary
    Life"

Note that an article (a, an, the) is capitalized only when it is part of the title or appears at the beginning of a sentence. Some newspapers and journals do not have an article on their masthead or title page; their titles, therefore, do not include an article. In these cases, if an article is needed to refer to the periodical, it should not be capitalized.

Her book is reviewed in the <u>Journal of Canadian Studies</u>, but she only subscribes to the <u>American Historical Review</u>. The <u>New York Times</u> broke the story.

When a word in a title is hyphenated, capitalize the letter after the hyphen if the second word is of equal importance to the first (this is usually the case). If the second only describes the first, or if the two words together are usually considered one word, do not capitalize the initial letter of the second word.

*Book Titles*
<u>Problem-Solving Strategies for Writing</u>
<u>A History of the Re-establishment of Order</u>

*Article Titles*
"Attitudes Toward Single-Parent Families"
"Neo-populism in Modern Development Theory"

For titles in reference lists, there are different styles of capitalization. In the social sciences and sciences, it is usual to capitalize only the first word, the first word after a colon or a dash, and all proper nouns in the titles of books and articles listed in the list of references. All major words in the titles of periodicals are capitalized.

## Italics

Underlining is the conventional way of indicating italics in typescript or manuscript. (Throughout this booklet, underlining has been used rather than italics, so you can be reminded of how the texts of your essays should look if you are unable to print them using computers that allow for italics.) The following are usually italicized in print or underlined in typescript or manuscript:

1. Titles in Text

   a) Italicize or underline the titles of published books, periodicals, pamphlets, plays, films, television and radio programs, long poems that have been published as books, collections of poetry, long musical compositions, dance works, paintings, sculptures, and classic works (except sacred texts or parts of sacred texts, which are neither underlined nor enclosed in quotation marks). You may choose either to underline spaces between words in a title or not to underline them, but be consistent. Enclose in quotation marks (do not underline) the titles of works that appear within larger works: the titles of articles and essays, chapters and sections of books (including introductions and prefaces), episodes of television and radio programs, single poems that are part of a collection of poetry, and songs or short musical compositions. Unpublished works like theses, dissertations, lectures, and speeches are usually placed in quotation marks as well.

*Books*
Red Earth: Revolution in a Sichuan Village
Le Rouge et le Noir

*Parts of Books*
"The Long Trek Home: Margaret Laurence's Stories"
(article in Margaret Laurence: An Appreciation)
"The Commercial Value of Imperialism"
(chapter in Imperialism)

*Periodicals*
Journal of Canadian Studies
Maclean's
The Globe and Mail

*Articles in Periodicals*
A recent Psychology Today article is entitled
    "How to Choose a President."
The Globe and Mail article "Mainstream AIDS Theory Challenged
    by Scientists" reports that the HIV virus is not the sole cause of AIDS.

*Pamphlet*
Towards Equity in Communication

*Play*
Waiting for Godot

*Film*
Triumph of the Will
The Great Train Robbery

*Works on Television and Radio*
    *Programs*                          *Episodes*
Star Trek: The Next Generation      "Detective Data"
Nature                              "Land of the Eagle"

*Poems*

| *Long Poems* | *Short poems* |
|---|---|
| The Waste Land | "The Journey of the Magi" |
| The Faerie Queene | "The Ruines of Time" |

*Collections of Poetry*
Songs of Innocence
Flowers for Hitler

*Musical Compositions and Recordings*

| *Long Musical Works* | *Short Musical Works* |
|---|---|
| The Well-Tempered Clavier | "Jesu, Joy of Man's Desiring" |
| The Sound of Music | "My Favorite Things" |
| Sgt. Pepper's Lonely Hearts Club Band | "Strawberry Fields Forever" |

Note that long musical compositions that are identified by form, number, and key rather than by name are not italicized or underlined: Beethoven's Symphony no. 9 in D minor or Beethoven's Ninth Symphony.

*Dance Works*
Swan Lake

*Art Works*

| *Paintings* | *Sculpture* |
|---|---|
| Starry Night | David |
| Guernica | Bird in Space |

Note that designations or names assigned to art works that are not actual titles are not italicized and are only capitalized if they are proper nouns: Mona Lisa, Venus.

*Classic Works*

| *Secular* | *Sacred* |
|---|---|
| Aeneid | Bible |
| | Book of the Dead |
| Iliad | Genesis |
| | Vedas |
| Odyssey | Koran |
| | Dead Sea Scrolls |

b) Underline the title as it appears on the title page. In some cases, particularly with newspapers and journals and certain classic works, the title may not include an initial definite article (the). Do not, therefore, include "the" as part of the title: write the Iliad, the Divine Comedy, Modern Philology. On the other hand, both capitalize and underline the initial definite article if it appears in the title: The Globe and Mail, The Canadian Forum.

c) Consult the "Documentation" section of this book to see how to capitalize and italicize titles in citations, notes, bibliographies, and lists of references. These titles are not treated the same as titles in text.

2. Foreign words and abbreviations that have not been thoroughly anglicized through usage:

| | | |
|---|---|---|
| Weltanschauung | legerdemain | a priori |
| mens rea | forte | et al. |
| mutatis mutandis | genre | per se |
| caveat emptor | aide-de-camp | vis-a-vis |

3. Genera, species, and varieties, but not divisions larger than genus (e.g., phylum, class, order, family):

| | |
|---|---|
| Homo sapiens | Primates |
| Acer saccharum | Aceraceae |

4. Quantity symbols and letters representing unknowns, but not unit symbols (SI symbols):

| *Quantity Symbols* | *Unit Symbols* | | |
|---|---|---|---|
| | (only examples are listed) | | |
| $x$ (an unknown quantity) | A (ampere) | km (kilometre) | N (newton) |
| $A$ (area) | cd (candela) | kW (kilowatt) | P (pascal) |
| $d$ (diameter) | cm (centimetre) | kn (knot) | s (second) |
| $h$ (height) | d (day) | L (litre) | t (tonne) |
| $l$ (length) | g (gram) | Mt (megatonne) | V (volt) |
| $m$ (mass) | ha (hectare) | m (metre) | W (watt) |
| $r$ (radius) | HZ (hertz) | mg (milligram) | |
| $t$ (time) | h (hour) | mL (millilitre) | |
| $v$ (velocity) | j (joule) | mm (millimetre) | |
| $V$ (volume) | K (kelvin) | mol (mole) | |
| $w$ (width) | kg(kilogram) | M (nautical mile) | |

5. Words that the writer wants to emphasize. Do not underline a word (or place it in quotation marks) simply because you feel it is not quite acceptable. If you underline for the sake of emphasis, do so only occasionally. If you underline or italicize a word in a quotation for emphasis, be sure to indicate that the emphasis is yours:

As Epictetus tells us, "If you wish to be a writer, <u>write</u>" (emphasis added).

## Numbers
In arts papers, numbers from one to one hundred and round numbers that can be expressed in two words are usually spelled out (for example, three hundred, nine million). Other numbers are usually given in figures:

The 138 survivors had walked over one thousand kilometres.

There are some exceptions to this rule, including numbers which express dates, numbers which express percentages, numbers used with a dollar symbol ($), and numbers with decimals:

Company profits between April 1 and June 30 were 17 percent higher than in the previous three months.

The average contribution was $7.00, which is 2.5 times greater than the average in 1972.

In scientific papers, use figures to express measurements and other numbers:

Each day 3 g of the substance was added to the food of the 16 animals in the second group.

In essays in both the arts and the sciences, avoid beginning a sentence with a number; if you must begin with a number, spell it out. Also, if figures must be used for some numbers in a sentence or paragraph, then use figures for all numbers applicable to the same category. In other words, consistency is important.

Use the following conventions when indicating inclusive numbers: for numbers 1 to 99, write both numbers in full (e.g., 31-36); for larger numbers (including dates), write the last two digits of the second number (e.g., 105-07, 1984-85) unless more digits are needed to describe the list clearly (e.g., 96-105, 1513-654).

### Expressions of Measurement

In arts papers, spell out units of measurement; do not use abbreviations even if a number is given.

```
Each man's pack weighed twenty-five kilograms or more.
(Do not write twenty-five kg.)
```

In scientific papers, units of measurement should be spelled out in full <u>unless</u> they are preceded by numbers:

```
The distance was measured in centimetres.

Copper wire, 18 cm long, was used to join these
points.
```

Use only standard abbreviations. Standard abbreviations for SI units (the International System of Units) can be found in the <u>Canadian Metric Practice Guide</u>, a publication of the Canadian Standards Association.

Confusion sometimes arises between "per cent" and "percentage." The first is used only when a particular measurement is given. In the sciences, "per cent" may be replaced by "%."[1]

```
There was an increase in volume of 112 per cent (or
112%).

The percentage of people who failed was low.
```

---

[1]We have spelled "per cent" as two words following the standard British spelling. The standard American spelling is "percent."

## Equations and Formulae

Distinguish equations and formulae from the text by isolating them on a line. Identify each one with a number (usually in parentheses at the right) so that you can refer to it easily later in the paper:

```
If "R" is the resistance and "d" the diameter, then
            R = k/d²                    (1)
for some constant "k."
```

## Tables and Illustrations

Tables, charts, graphs, maps, diagrams, and illustrations—all of these graphic displays help to sort and summarize information in an essay or report. A few clear, well-chosen graphics can eliminate the need for lengthy description and can make complex information easier for your reader to comprehend. In certain disciplines, such as Biology and Anthropology, even the act of drawing can work as a learning tool to heighten observational skills which are essential to the accurate description of phenomena.

If possible and practical, produce your own graphics because those you create will be made to relate specifically to your paper's purpose. If, however, you find you must use graphics from other sources, be certain that they fit the context of your paper and that your sources are documented (see "Citing Graphic Sources," page 29).

### 1. The Stages of Graphic Work

Producing graphics for an essay requires planning and preparation. The time spent at the planning stage can save time in the long run and reduce the potential for errors in your work. Most graphics begin with a rough pencil draft. From this rough draft a final draft might be produced manually or by computer. Even though computer programs can produce drawings and organize data, it is still your task to decide which graph, chart, or table illustrates the data best. Manually produced graphics may be begun as neat pencil drawing and then be taken to a carefully finished ink illustration. In some cases, good pencil copies are acceptable for exercises and lab reports.

There are roughly four stages in the production of a graphic for use in an academic paper:

sorting data,
designing the graphic,
choosing the best computer-designed graphic,
or
drawing an accurate pencil copy, and
producing the final ink copy.

## 2. Methods

After choosing the information you wish to display in the graphic, you must choose the appropriate method to display it. Do not force data into table form when the information could be better shown in a graph, or on a chart, or explained within the text. In the design stage, you should work out proper scales and layout of the graphic. Aim for clarity in your work: remove material that obscures the main idea. Produce an accurate pencil copy, and check it for errors before proceeding to the final stage of inking your illustration. The final copy should be neat, clean, and uncluttered.

Graphics must be understandable: the information they contain must be simple, clear, and accurate, and the display format must be legible. Several simple, single-idea graphics often present information much more clearly than one graphic which is cluttered and overly detailed.

## 3. Lettering

Variation in script and font can enhance readability. A computer-assisted design will allow you to choose the lettering options of the software program. Hand lettering is acceptable for most student exercises and lab reports, but it is important that the lettering be neat, evenly spaced, and legible.

## 4. Labels, Captions, and Legends

Every graphic should include:

a label,
a caption (title),
legend (optional), and
an acknowledgement of its source (if necessary).

a) Labels: Graphics, including graphs, charts, maps, and illustrations are usually given the label "Figure" and numbered consecutively within the text (e.g., Figure 1, Figure 2, or Fig. 1, Fig. 2). Photographs or reproductions of art works may be labelled "Plate" or "Illus." ("illustration") and numbered. Likewise, tables are labelled and numbered consecutively in the order in which they appear in the paper (e.g., Table 1, Table 2). The label is aligned with the left margin of the graphic and may be placed either above or directly below it.

b) Captions: A caption entitling the illustration is placed two spaces below the label. The first word and all other words except conjunctions, articles, and prepositions are capitalized. It ends with a period.

c) Legends: The caption is often directly followed by a brief explanatory statement called a legend. It may contain one or more sentences, or it may be a phrase or fragment, in which case it may be written in the same form as the caption. Both caption and legend may be placed either above or below the illustration.

Table 1 (the label)

Metropolitan Zoo Attendance. (the caption)
Number of Visitors over a Five-Year Period. (the legend)

| | |
|---|---|
| 1979 | 100,678 |
| 1980 | 129,386 |
| 1981 | 131,890 |
| 1982 | 130,920 |
| 1983 | 134,521 |

The label, caption, and legend should reveal enough information about the graphic to make it self-explanatory. In other words, your reader must be able to understand your graphic without having to make constant reference to your text.

### 5. Citing Graphic Sources

Any graphic which is not your own must be properly acknowledged in the documentation style which is specific to your discipline. If you have produced your own graphic based on information from another source, you must acknowledge the source of the information. Failure to cite a graphic which is not your own, either in whole or in part, is regarded as plagiarism.

The use of photocopies or photographically reproduced graphics from an original source without permission may be an infringement of copyright. It is preferable that you produce your own work whenever possible. However, in an unpublished, undergraduate research paper, one-time use of photocopied material for personal research purposes is generally permissible provided that the source is properly acknowledged. If you are using photocopies in your paper, use only clear, clean copies. Crop and mount them neatly as you would any other graphic. To avoid possible confusion, remove the original labels and assign labels which conform to the labelling and enumeration you have chosen for your paper (for example, Figure 1 or Table 1).

When a table or illustration is not your creation, a note must accompany it to document its source. Acknowledgement of the source is usually given in one of two ways: 1) placed in parentheses, immediately following the legend, or 2) placed immediately below the lower left-hand corner of the table or illustration. Complete bibliographical information must be supplied in this source information: the word "Source," followed by a colon, then by the citation which is presented in the same way as it would be if it were an unabridged footnote to a source. Since the method for citing a source varies among disciplines, it is advisable to consult the "List of Documentation Methods by Academic Discipline" in this book, to ask your instructor, or to follow the format given in a current journal in your field of study in order to obtain the accepted documentation method.

Citations for graphics need not be repeated in a list of references, a list of works cited, or in a bibliography.

Examine the format of the following example.

Fig 6.7

An Example of the Evolution of Lake Ice, Including Snow Cover. Seasonal development of the winter lake cover of Big Cedar Lake, 1976-77. This diagram shows the development of the ice and snow cover for a small lake in the Kawartha region. Note the sequence of cover development (black ice followed by snow accumulation followed by white ice), and the rapid melting of the white ice cover with the removal of the snowcover in early March, demonstrating the insulating properties of snow.

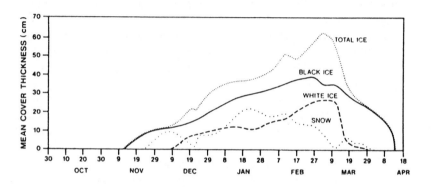

Source: Peter Adams and Colin Taylor, eds., <u>Peterborough and the Kawarthas</u> (Peterborough, ON: Heritage, 1985) 87.

## 6. Explanatory Notes

Notes to tables are placed at the end of the table and may be given a lower-case letter designation to avoid confusing number symbols with numerical data in the table. Alternatively, you may use symbols (*, **, ***) to alert readers to refer to explanatory notes that are situated beneath a table or illustration, or at the bottom of the page. Symbols to notes are usually placed in a superscript position. Begin a new series of notes for each table.

## 7. Placement of Graphics

Graphics, including maps and photographs, should be placed as close as possible to the first reference to them in the paper. If the graphic is larger than half a page, mount it on a separate page, and place it directly after the page of text that refers to the graphic. Number the graphic page consecutively with the pagination of the essay. Sometimes you will want to add a series of graphics at the end of your essay; in this case, label them to conform with your already established sequence, and number the pages consecutively with the pagination of the essay.

# _____PART III: QUOTATIONS_____

## THE PROPER USE OF SOURCES

You can support your ideas and make your essay lively and interesting with well-chosen quotations. Because quotations are first-hand evidence of the contributors to your thought, quoting your sources is desirable, even expected. This is particularly so when writing a humanities research paper. Rather than detracting from your work, well-chosen quotations add to it, giving your argument validity and support. You should be careful, however, to use quotations sparingly, because using them to support your ideas is one thing, allowing them to take control of your paper is quite another. Your essay belongs to you; resist the temptation of letting the authors of your sources speak for you. Most of the paper should contain your discussion and analysis, while carefully selected quotations (as well as accurate paraphrase and succinct summary) provide useful contextual information and supportive data.

### Quoting from Primary and Secondary Sources
Quotations in an essay come from either primary or secondary sources. Often the distinction between the two kinds of sources is not immediately apparent and depends on the context in which sources are used and the purpose for which they are used. Nevertheless, it is important to be able to distinguish between these two kinds of sources when researching, and when quoting from your research material.

1. Primary Sources
Primary sources might be public records, statistics, maps, manuscripts, government documents, letters, minutes, newspaper announcements, charts, first-hand accounts, and original works of literature. The "primary" nature of this material is its originality. Generally, it is information, artifact, or creative writing without any accompanying interpretation. If you are writing an essay about <u>Great Expectations</u>, then the primary source is that novel, not texts of literary criticism of that novel. However, if your essay is about literary criticisms of <u>Great Expectations</u>, then the criticisms would be considered primary sources. In the study of history, the primary source provides the raw evidence for analysis, but, in the study of historiography, the histories themselves are primary sources. When you quote from primary sources, you do so to support your original, or "first-hand", observations and arguments.

## 2. Secondary Sources

Secondary sources are most often articles, editorials, textbooks, and books that interpret other texts and works of literature, data, ideas, or events. The information they yield has been observed or gathered and interpreted by someone other than you; you receive it "second-hand." When your essay is centred on primary research, you are a first commentator, an original responder; if your essay is based on secondary material, your essay is a response to other commentators and researchers—you are entering into a dialogue with them and commenting on primary material indirectly. You must be able to assess your sources critically. If you rely too heavily on quotations from secondary sources to carry the meaning of your essay, you run the risk of shifting the burden of proof from your thesis to that of an outside commentator. You might even compound the errors or biases of the secondary source. Nevertheless, quotations from secondary sources are appropriate in some instances, particularly when you want to summon a recognized authority to strengthen a point you are making, a point that the reader might question or refute. You are, in effect, using the secondary source to persuade your reader: you are saying "I have come to this conclusion and so has this learned scientist (historian, critic, or theorist)."

### Quoting for Style

Sometimes it is style or eloquence that prompts you to quote a phrase or passage. In this instance, you quote an author because he or she has expressed important ideas in the most clear and concise form possible, or with particular flair.

### Careful Quoting: Integrated, Appropriate, Accurate

If your quotations are to be effective, they must be an integral part of your essay. Resist the temptation to throw in a quotation merely because it sounds impressive and has, you feel, <u>something</u> to do with your subject. Work quoted material—verse or prose, short or long passages—into <u>the meaning</u> of your own sentences in order to avoid any disjointedness with the expression of your thought.

Focus on your meaning to decide if a chosen quotation is appropriate or not. When you have decided that the quotation fits your meaning, re-check the quotation in its original context to make certain that you have preserved the meaning intended by its author.

Ensure that the quotation corresponds exactly with the wording, spelling, and punctuation of the original. Any editorial changes that you make to the quotation must be indicated by ellipsis dots or square brackets. Always indicate a quotation by using quotation marks to open and close the borrowed passage, or (for longer extracts as described below) by indenting and using single- or double-spacing.

Your prose should introduce the quotation and should flow into the quotation, both in grammatical form and in meaning. Unless its significance is perfectly clear in the context of your essay, the quotation should be accompanied by comments that provide your reader with all relevant interpretation.

### Quoting Prose

1. Short Quotations: Prose quotations of four typed lines or less are usually incorporated into the text of the essay and are enclosed within quotation marks. Follow these guidelines:

a) **Integrating Quotations:** The quotation should fit into your sentence or paragraph as an integral part of your language and meaning[1]:

> Robert Seton-Watson, the English historian, joined the fight against the pretentious use of language when he stressed that "[i]n our Victorian dislike of the practice of calling a spade a bloody shovel, it is not necessary to go to the opposite extreme of calling it an agricultural implement."

It would be incorrect and confusing to write:

> Robert Seton-Watson, the English historian, "In our Victorian dislike of the practice of calling a spade a bloody shovel, it is not necessary to

---

[1]Note that in an essay, all quotations are documented, in an endnote, footnote, or in parentheses, immediately following the quotation. No documentation has been created for the examples given here. For correct documentation format, see Part IV.

go to the opposite extreme of calling it an
agricultural implement."

b) **Punctuation to Introduce Quotations:** Short quotations may be
worked into the construction of your sentences` without any
introductory or additional punctuation:

The bodies of these Indians were not painted in
brilliant colours but rather "in the subdued
colours provided by earth and rock."

Another way to introduce a short quotation is with a colon preceded
by an independent clause. The clause introduces the idea or the
context of the quotation which follows the colon:

Hedley Bull is quite clear on this point: "We are
accustomed, in the modern world, to contrast war
between states with peace between states; but the
historical alternative to war between states was
more ubiquitous violence."

**Punctuation to Close Quotations:** Periods or commas at the
close of a quotation are placed within the quotation marks unless
parenthetical material (for instance, documentation) follows the
quotation, in which case the comma or period is placed after the
closing parenthesis. All other marks of punctuation are placed
outside the quotation marks except when they are part of quoted
material.[2] Note the following examples:

1. Ultimately, we see King Lear as a victim, "a man
   more sinned against than sinning."
2. "The reproductive capacity of the blue whale was
   the lowest of all baleen species," reports Small.
3. "The reproductive capacity of the blue whale,"
   reports Small, "was the lowest of all baleen
   species."

---

[2]For a full discussion of punctuating quotations, see Karen Taylor et al. Clear, Correct,
Creative: A Handbook for Writers of Academic Prose (Peterborough, ON: Academic
Skills Centre, Trent U, 1991) 243-255.

4. The 1971 Evaluation Task Force concluded that "Opportunities for Youth was a case of too little spread too thinly" (Doern and Wilson, p. 150).
5. What does Hunter mean by "haphazard urban agglomeration"?
6. Wood begins by asking "What is an ethnic group?"

c) **Quotations within Quotations:** Use single quotation marks if you have already used double marks around the entire passage:

> From then on "Balfour was no longer Knox's 'faithful brother,' but 'blasphemous Balfour,' the 'principal misguider now of Scotland,' who above all others ought to be abhorred."

d) **Deleting Sections of a Quotation:** Occasionally the original version of the quotation you are using will not be perfectly suited to your needs. If you wish to omit part of a quotation, do so by an ellipsis mark consisting of three spaced periods in addition to any period marking the end of a sentence. Check that your deletion has not altered the meaning of the quotation:

> "Previous fossil discoveries there . . . include trilobites of middle Cambrian age . . . ."

e) **Insertions:** If you wish to insert a word or more of explanation, or a word or punctuation mark to make the quotation grammatically correct, do so by enclosing the added words or punctuation marks in square brackets:

> "[T]he task [of the McDonald Commission] is to investigate the alleged illegal activities of the RCMP."

(Insert the square brackets in ink if necessary; do not use parentheses.)

f) **Accuracy:** If you wish to indicate that your quotation is accurate even though its spelling or logic is faulty, place the word "sic" (which means "thus" or "so") within square brackets following the error to tell your reader that your rendition of the quotation is consistent with the original:

These children "gave evidence that their ability to put evemts [sic] in sequence was severely impaired."

The rules that govern all quoting in general, and the use of ellipsis dots, square brackets, and "sic" in particular, are to preserve the sense and integrity of the original passage.

2. Long Quotations: Use longer excerpts sparingly. You can often make your point better with a short selection than with a longer one, and your reader will be less likely to lose the thread of your argument. However, long quotations are sometimes necessary to preserve accuracy and completeness of meaning, and if you choose to quote a passage of more than four lines, indent it and use single-spacing or double-spacing, depending on the style required. **Quotation marks are not used unless they appear within the text of the quoted material.** Follow the general rules for punctuation and accuracy that are covered in b, c, d, e, f, above. In the example below, note the use of the colon after the writer's independent introductory clause and before the quoted passage.

Rea and McLeod outline the three fundamental concepts of socialism:

First, socialists have desired to substitute public ownership for private ownership of the principal means of production. Second, socialists have emphasized equality and have sought to establish equality of opportunity, which, they maintain, is neither present nor possible under capitalism. Third, since the 1930's, socialists have emphasized the concept of "economic planning" and have wished to substitute planning for the so-called "automatic," or "self-regulating," market.

Make certain to introduce the quotation so that it is linked clearly and smoothly with the thought of your essay. After the quotation, make sure that you supply any needed explanations or comments on the quotation. Do not assume that your reader will interpret the quotation exactly as you have.

## Quoting Poetry

1. Short Quotations: Verse quotations of a single line or less should be incorporated (in quotation marks) into the grammar and meaning of your text. Selections of two lines may be incorporated in the same way, but with the lines separated by a slash (/):

An example of alliteration occurs in the lines "And jealous of the listening air/They steel their way from stair to stair."

2. Long Quotations: Longer quotations should be centred on the page, spaced, and set line for line as they are printed in the original. They should also follow as closely as possible the arrangement of words, lines, and punctuation of the original. Quotation marks are not used, but are retained if they appear in the original text of the poem.

> The hand which still held Juan's, by degrees
>     Gently, but palpably confirmed its grasp,
> As if it said, "Detain me, if you please";
>     Yet there's no doubt she only meant to clasp
> His fingers with a pure Platonic squeeze.

Omitting a line, several lines or stanzas is indicated by a line of ellipsis dots. For example, a quotation from <u>The Rime of the Ancient Mariner</u> by Samuel Taylor Coleridge might look like this:

> It is an ancient Mariner,
> And he stoppeth one of three.
> "By thy long grey beard and glittering eye,
> Now wherefore stopp'st thou me? ["]
>
> ......................................
>
> He holds him with his glittering eye—
> The Wedding-Guest stood still,
> And listens like a three years' child:
> The Mariner hath his will.

Be cautioned that too many long quotations can make it difficult for the reader to follow your line of reasoning, and block quotations strung together without introductions, analyses, or explanations may cause you to lose your reader entirely.

### Attribution

Attribution allows a writer to acknowledge properly sources in the body of the text as well as in the documentation. Readers often need to know the author and other circumstances in order to interpret and evaluate a quotation accurately. Even when complete documentation is supplied, the reader may find it necessary to search for useful circumstantial information at the source. This circumstantial information should be supplied in the text of the essay. Note the serious problem that would arise if a student were to write:

> The claim has been made that, "if one consults only
> absolute figures, unmarried persons seem to commit
> suicide less than married ones" (Durkheim, 1951:171).

Without the necessary attribution, the reader might believe that Durkheim made this claim. An accurate citation with correct attribution would read:

> In 1897, Emile Durkheim used systematic statistical
> investigation to disprove the claim of Bertillon Sr.
> that "if one consults only absolute figures, unmarried
> persons seem to commit suicide less than married ones"
> (Durkheim, 1951:171).

The claim is now attributed to its correct author by naming him in the text.

# THE IMPROPER USE OF SOURCES:
# PLAGIARISM

Plagiarism—passing off someone else's words or thoughts as your own—is a serious academic offence. The student who plagiarizes may expect to receive at least a reprimand and possibly a failure in the essay or course, depending upon the circumstances and the kind of plagiarism involved.

The worst kind of plagiarism, of course, is submitting an essay written in whole or in part by someone else. Even a short passage copied directly constitutes plagiarism unless the student encloses the passage in quotation marks and acknowledges the source. But the student who changes only the odd word in someone else's sentences is also (perhaps unwittingly) committing plagiarism, as is one who relies heavily on secondary sources for the argument, organization, and main points of his or her paper. Even the properly documented paraphrasing of someone else's writing constitutes plagiarism if the paraphrase contains phrasing from the original that is not enclosed in quotation marks.

Remember, as well, that you should not copy lines or paragaraphs verbatim from your own essays, essays that you have previously submitted and for which you have received a grade. Even though the ideas expressed in these lines belong to you, you are not free to quote sections of your old essays without any documentation. Because your ideas will continue to develop throughout your university career, it is understandable that some of your themes and concepts are likely to resurface in papers dealing with the same or similar subjects. Nevertheless, the expression of these thoughts and ideas should always be revised to fit every new context.

Naturally, a well-conceived and thoroughly researched essay will make use of facts and ideas found in a number of sources and from time to time will quote those facts or ideas in their original wording. This is equally true of other forms of writing: lab reports, summary and precis assignments, problem-solving calculations, and computer programs. Quoting and paraphrasing material is permissible and scholarly provided you indicate when you are quoting directly and when you are paraphrasing, and provided you acknowledge your debt to your sources—in a footnote or in a citation within the text—each time you depart from your own prose.

There are, however, times when you need not acknowledge a source. When facts are well known or when ideas are commonly held in a discipline, there is no need to document their source. Often, the original source of this type of information is either unknown, widely known, or inconsequential. For example, you need not document that American federal politics is based on a two-party system. Plagiarism occurs when facts or ideas not commonly known or held in the field are presented in an essay without the proper format and documentation. When in the least doubt, document the source. You can avoid committing plagiarism unwittingly by reading widely in the discipline and by using good research and notetaking techniques (see "Researching the Essay").

To illustrate, suppose you wanted to quote from the following passage from <u>Modern England</u> by R.K. Webb:

By the middle of Victoria's reign, therefore, the Established Church was dominated by two groups who earlier in the century had been minorities— the Tractarians and their Anglo-Catholic heirs, the Evangelicals. Both the Tractarians and the Evangelicals agreed that the enemy was religious liberalism, but beyond that, there was no possibility of accommodation between them.

Plagiarism occurs whenever you borrow words and ideas without documentation. Thus the following use of the above material is unacceptable:

The Established Church was undergoing a marked change by the middle of Victoria's reign. It was dominated by two groups, the Tractarians and the Evangelicals, and both of these former religious minorities agreed that the enemy was religious liberalism.

The correct form would be to attribute this information to Webb and document it appropriately:

```
R.K. Webb points out that "[b]y the middle of
Victoria's reign . . . the Established Church was
dominated by two groups who earlier in the century
had been minorities—the Tractarians and their Anglo-
Catholic heirs, the Evangelicals. Both . . . agreed
that the enemy was religious liberalism . . . ."
```

The following excerpt is contained in an entry on Sigmund Freud in the third edition of Benet's Reader's Encyclopedia.

Freud postulated the existence of three internal forces that govern a person's psychic life: (1) the id, the instinctual force of life—unconscious, uncontrollable, and isolated; (2) the ego, the executive force that has contact with the real world; (3) the super-ego, the governing force, or moral conscience, that seeks to control and direct the ego into socially acceptable patterns of behaviour.

An inexperienced writer, incorrectly assuming that essays are simply a compilation of facts gleaned from various sources, might write the following without documentation:

```
Freud claimed that people had three internal forces
that governed their psychic life: the id, which is
instinctual; the ego, which is the executive force
based on reality; and the super-ego, which is the
governing force directing the ego into acceptable
patterns of behaviour.
```

This is an example of plagiarism because phrases and syntactical patterns are borrowed directly from the original without any attempt at paraphrase or interpretation. The writer could have avoided plagiarism with proper quoting and documentation:

```
Freud revolutionized the study of the human
personality when he "postulated the existence of
three forces that govern a person's psychic life:
(1) the id, the instinctual force of life—unconscious,
uncontrollable, and isolated; (2) the ego, the
executive force that has contact with the real world;
(3) the super-ego, the governing force, or moral
conscience, that seeks to control and direct the
ego into socially acceptable patterns of behaviour"
(Benet's Reader's Encyclopedia).
```

(In this example, note that no page number need be given because the encylopaedia entries are listed alphabetically.)

If a student wrote that "the three psychic forces first described by Sigmund Freud were the id, the ego, and the super-ego," it would not be considered an act of plagiarism because Freud's concepts are now considered common knowledge, and this information can be found in many different sources. Using the words "psychic," "id," "ego," and "super-ego" is, in this instance, not plagiarism.

### Paraphrasing

Paraphrasing material and incorporating it into your own text comes naturally when you have read and researched extensively. However, this natural tendency to express the ideas of others in your own words should be exercised with great care, both for the language and for the documentation. When paraphrasing, refer to your notes and to the original source, if necessary, to make certain that you are true to the author's meaning. When you express someone else's ideas in your own words, it is important that you do not distort this meaning. Skilful paraphrase allows you to remain fully in control of the expression of your thesis while pointing out the ideas of others.

Read the following passage and study the example of incorrect and of correct paraphrase. The original passage is taken from a review, written by Michael J. Sidnell, of the 1991 Stratford Festival in the April 1992 edition of the Journal of Canadian Studies. The passage describes the acting ability of Brian Bedford in The School for Wives:

It was Bedford <u>suprême</u>. He didn't just play to the
gallery, he found somebody up there to point to, and
another collaborative spectator in the stalls below.
No part of the house was unworked, no occasion
neglected for double takes, lip-pursings, poses,
and pauses—no manner of signifying was too coarse for
him, and his audience adored him for the pains he took
to please them. They would gladly have given this
Arnolphe the girl, the money and, of course, the
palm.

A plagiarized description of Bedford's performance follows:

Bedford's audiences adored him for his acting ability.
He went to any length to please them—he worked the
house from the gallery to the stalls below—with double
takes, lip-pursing, poses, and pauses.

To document this paraphrase would not save it from committing
unabashed plagiarism. The writer has "lifted" the language directly from
the original and has scarcely processed it for the purpose of his essay.

Compare the previous paraphrase with this acceptable one:

Bedford was well known and appreciated for his ability
to engage his audiences. The characters he played may
have been created as blackguards and buffoons but he
played them with humour, as a joyful gift to the
audience. Michael Sidnell's review of <u>The School for
Wives</u> describes the energy and dramatic flair that
Bedford brought to the role of Arnolphe and won for
him the full acclaim—even the love—of his audience
(153).

In this version, the writer remains in control of the ideas expressed, while
the paraphrase serves as an example of a point that the essayist is making.

# PART IV:
## DOCUMENTATION

### DOCUMENTATION—GENERAL INFORMATION

**Why Document?**

Documentation of references, whether by parenthetical citation or footnoting, serves three main purposes. First, it can increase the credibility of the argument presented. When the reader can see that a fact comes from a reliable source, or that a conclusion was reached not only by the author of the paper, but also by a reputable scholar in the field, the reader is more likely to be persuaded of the overall argument. Secondly, documentation allows the reader of your essay to locate material you have used to check its accuracy, read it in its original context, or seek further information. Finally, of course, documentation is quite simply a way of acknowledging sources and avoiding plagiarism.

**What to Document**

Every thoroughly researched essay will make use of facts and ideas found in a number of sources. Whether these facts and ideas are quoted directly or paraphrased, they must be acknowledged.

The difficulty in documentation lies in deciding what must be documented: sometimes every fact and idea in a research paper seems to originate in another source. Keep in mind that there is no need to acknowledge facts that are well known or ideas that are commonly held within a discipline. For example, in a Canadian politics essay, there would be no need to document that Canadian federal politics is based on constitutional democracy. However, if you are in doubt as to whether a fact or idea is known or held by only a few writers in the field, or is generally accepted, document the source.

If you keep in mind the purposes of documentation—to increase the credibility of your argument by showing your reader the origins of facts and ideas, to enable your reader to find the material you have used, and to give credit where credit is due—it should be relatively easy to decide what to document.

**How to Document**

Because your reader must be able to locate the material that you have cited quickly and easily, your documentation must be precise and concise. At a minimum, the reader will need to know the author's name, the title of the work, and the publishing details (the publisher, and the place and date of publication). If you are referring to a piece which is part of a larger publication—for instance, an article in a book or journal—then you must provide information not only about the piece itself but also about the publication in which it is found (e.g., the name of the book and its editor, the volume and date of the journal). Depending on the method of documentation used and the nature of the source, you may also have to supply additional information, such as page references, so that the source can be located with a minimum of effort. As we have advised in the section "Researching the Essay," this information should be recorded on bibliographic cards as you research so that it will be readily available when you compile the list of works cited or bibliography.

Because certain information is key, documentation must be as streamlined as possible to prevent the reader from being distracted by superfluous details. For instance, when citing a publisher, it is not always necessary to write "The Butterworth Group of Companies"; "Butterworth" may give the reader all the information needed. Similarly, when the publisher is a university press, you may not need to write "Carleton University Press"; "Carleton UP" is usually sufficient. As you use Notes, pay particular attention to the concise manner in which information is documented and attempt to imitate that style whenever possible.

### Methods of Documentation

Because methods of documentation vary from discipline to discipline, it is essential to find out which format you are expected to use. This edition of Notes on the Preparation of Essays in the Arts and Sciences brings together the information that undergraduate students need most frequently when documenting papers for courses in a variety of disciplines—in the humanities, in the social sciences, and in the natural sciences. Although rules of documentation vary from discipline to discipline and from subject to subject, there are essentially three principal methods for citing and listing your sources:

**Method One**: Footnoting

**Method Two**: Parenthetical Documentation

**Method Three:** Number-Reference Method

Guidelines for documentation in humanities disciplines, which use both the footnoting and the parenthetical documentation methods, are based on the 1988 edition of the MLA Handbook for Writers of Research Papers. Guidelines for documentation in the social sciences, which use the parenthetical documentation method primarily, are based on the 1986 Publication Manual of the American Psychological Association. While there is no single model for documentation in the natural sciences, we have followed the form generally recommended, that described by the Council of Biology Editors in the CBE Style Manual.

The sections which follow will explain more fully these three main methods of documentation and demonstrate their use in different subject areas. Method One--Footnoting (used primarily in humanities disciplines such as history and classical studies) is followed by Method Two--Parenthetical Documentation. Method Two is subdivided into two relatively distinct styles: Style A (used primarily in humanities such as English literature and philosophy) and Style B (used primarily in social sciences such as psychology, biology and political science). Method Three, the Number-Reference Method, is used primarily in natural sciences such as chemistry, physics, and mathematics. Part V lists the documentation methods preferred by academic disciplines and indicates some of the variations that occur within styles depending on the field of study. There may be times when you will want to consult a more extensive or a more specific style guide. A number of these are listed on page 145 of this text. If you are uncertain about which method, style, or guide to follow, consult your course syllabus, your instructor, or a leading journal in your field of study. In all cases, it is important to adopt one method and to use it consistently throughout your paper.

# DOCUMENTATION USING THE FOOTNOTING METHOD

The footnoting method uses short notes (located either at the bottom of each page of the essay or on a separate page at the end of the essay) to document sources. Generally this method includes a "Bibliography," that is, a page or pages attached at the end of the essay that list all the works cited and all those consulted, or, in some cases, only those works cited. In this method, complete publication information is included in the first reference to a source (in a footnote) as well as in the bibliography.

## When to Use the Footnoting Method

For many years, the footnoting method was standard for documenting sources, and many schools, disciplines, and scholarly journals in the humanities continue to recommend it. It is the preferred method when authors and readers want full references to relate closely with the text. In disciplines such as history and philosophy, this documentation method has important scholarly implications. Having this information on the same page as the text (or in endnotes that can be placed beside the text as one reads) helps to communicate important information to the reader without that information impinging on the focus of the writer's thesis or on the flow of the text. In addition, the information in the note often makes more readily available important contextual material that helps the reader to detect the bias of the source, to evaluate the source, to determine the validity of cited facts and ideas, and to assign credit or blame where it is due.

## How to Footnote/Endnote

A footnote appears at the bottom of the same page as the citation or quotation appears in the text of the essay. Alternatively, the footnotes may be listed on separate pages immediately following the essay and any appendices, and before the bibliography. These footnotes are referred to as endnotes and are entitled "Notes," but in format and style they are identical to footnotes. They are footnotes, but in this case, they are footnotes numbered sequentially at the "foot" or end of the paper.

Footnotes placed at the end of an essay have the advantage over footnotes placed at the bottom of the page in that space is not limited: the page of text need not be adjusted so that the notes fit at the bottom. On the other hand, placing footnotes at the bottom of the page allows both writer and reader to have immediate reference to the documentation that accompanies the text of each page. Because computer programs, such as WordPerfect, space and format footnotes automatically with each corresponding page of text, this style of footnoting is becoming preferable to listing notes at the end of the essay.

## Numbering

In both endnoting and footnoting, text to be documented is indicated by small arabic superscript numbers (e.g., [1],[2],[3]), and the notes are listed consecutively at the foot of each page or at the end of the paper by corresponding superscript numbers. In the text of the essay, the arabic numerals are placed after the end punctuation of the sentence in which the cited material is incorporated. However, if there is any possibility that paraphrased material might be confused with your original material, the number should be placed within the sentence immediately following the cited material, or, in the case of quoted material, immediately following the closing quotation mark. As a general rule, the reference number should follow all punctuation marks except the dash.

As Bismarck once remarked, the next great war in Europe would be set off by "some damned foolish thing in the Balkans."[1]

"Some damned foolish thing in the Balkans," Bismarck once remarked, would set off the next great European war.[1]

"Some damned foolish thing in the Balkans,"[1] Bismarck once remarked, would set off the next great European war, and that thing was Serb nationalism, which was embodied in two famous political organizations founded at the time of the Bosnian annexation crisis and the Balkan wars: Narodna Odbrana and Ujedinjenje ili Smrt.[2]

Care must be taken to make certain that the reference numbers in the text refer to the appropriately numbered notes at the foot of the page or in the list of endnotes. If notes are added or deleted during revision, the writer must remember to re-number the footnotes/endnotes to reflect the changes made.

Numbers should never be repeated in the text to refer to the same footnote; instead, create a subsequent note directing the reader to "see note (number) above."

Do not use a footnote reference number in headings or titles. Use an asterisk (*) instead to refer the reader to an explanatory note situated at the bottom of the page, or, in a case where the writer wants to document a reference made on the title page of an essay, at the bottom of the first page of the text. This note should contain all the needed documentation, and this documentation is not listed in the bibliography.

Illustrations such as charts, graphs, or tables are not footnoted with the text. Notes to this type of material appear below the illustration, and are not included in the list of footnotes/endnotes. See pages 28-31 for examples.

**Spacing**

Leave plenty of room for footnotes. Do not squeeze them in at the bottom of the page. Separate the first footnote on each page from the last line of the text by quadruple-spacing (two double-spaces) and, if you wish, by a line ruled part way across the page. Leave a one-inch space from the bottom of the page. Many computer programs will space and number footnotes automatically.

Endnotes are listed on pages following the text of the essay. These pages are numbered consecutively with the text. On the first page, the title "Notes" is centred and placed one inch from the top of the page. Leave two blank lines before entering the first note.

Whether you use endnotes or footnotes, each reference should be treated as if it were a separate paragraph. That is to say, the first line should be indented five spaces from the margin and should begin with the superscript arabic number, without punctuation. The second and subsequent lines of each note are typed flush with the left margin. If you use endnotes, double-space between notes, and single-space or double-space within notes. If you use footnotes, single-space within the footnotes but double-space between them.

## The First Footnote to a Source

### STANDARD FORM

The **first footnote** to a source contains full bibliographic information, while **second and subsequent footnotes** to that source abbreviate and delete certain bibliographic material. (Please see pages 68-71 for variations and accepted abbreviations of standard form.)

### First References to Published Books: Guidelines

In a footnote/endnote that is a first reference to a published book, information is normally arranged in the following order. This list is comprehensive, and you will find that not all items of information in the list apply to every book.

1. Author's name, in normal order and as it appears on the title page
2. Title of the part of the book used (e.g., article within book, poem).
3. Title of the book, as it appears on the title page.
4. Name of the editor, translator, or compiler.
5. Edition, if other than the first.
6. Volume number(s).
7. Series name.
8. Place of publication.
9. Publisher's name.
10. Date of publication.
11. Page number(s).
12. Supplementary bibliographical material, in complete sentences.

This information should be arranged and punctuated in accordance with the following example:

¹Fred Flintstone, Barney Rubble, and Betty Rubble, "Ode to Wilma," <u>The Collected Works of Fred Flintstone: A Tribute to Neolithic Creativity</u>, ed. Arnold A. Anthropologist, 2nd ed., vol. 4 of 5 vols., Pre-Historic Verse 17 (New York: Cambrian P, 1984) 18. In 2100, Cambrian plans to publish a commemorative edition that will include an introduction by Bam Bam.

### Second and Subsequent References

In second and subsequent references, use a shortened form of the first note. Give only enough information to identify the work. Usually the author's last name followed by the appropriate page numbers is sufficient:

> ³⁴Brody 19.

If two or more works by the same author are referred to in the essay, you should give a shortened form of the title after the author's name:

> ³⁵Dickens, <u>David Copperfield</u> 160.

> ³⁶Dickens, <u>Pickwick</u> 245.

### First References to Published Books and Sections of Books: Examples

*Books—Variations of Author*

a) **A book with a single author:**

> ¹Hugh Brody, <u>The People's Land: Eskimos and Whites in the Eastern Arctic</u> (Harmondsworth, Eng.: Penguin, 1975) 68.

b) **A book with a single author and an editor or translator, when references are to the author, not the editor:** The editor's name, preceded by "ed." (or the translator's name, preceded by "trans.") is given after the title.

> ²Charles Dickens, <u>The Personal History of David Copperfield</u>, ed. Trevor Blount (Harmondsworth, Eng.: Penguin, 1966) 154-56.

c) **A book with an editor or translator, when references are to the edited material: the introduction, notes, editorial decisions regarding layout, etc.:**

> [3]R.D. Olling and M.W. Westmacott, eds., <u>The Confederation Debate: The Constitution in Crisis</u> (Toronto: Kendall/Hunt, 1980) 55.

d) **A book with either two or three authors:** The first author's name, as well as other authors' names, is given in standard order (first name or initials followed by surname).

> [5]Paul F. Langer and Joseph Zasloff, <u>North Vietnam and the Pathet Lao: Partners in the Struggle for Laos</u> (Cambridge, MA: Harvard UP, 1970) 6.

e) **A book with more than three authors:** In the note, the first author only may be given, followed by "et al." ("and others"):

> [6]Mary Field Belenky, et al., <u>Women's Ways of Knowing: The Development of Self, Voice, and Mind</u> (New York: Basic, 1986) 96.

If only one author is cited in the note, it is usual to cite all the authors in the bibliography. If the essay has no bibliography, it is usual to cite all the authors in the first footnote:

> [7]Mary Field Belenky, Blythe McVicker Clinchy, Nancy Rule Goldberg, and Jill Mattuck Tarule, <u>Women's Ways of Knowing: The Development of Self, Voice, and Mind</u> (New York: Basic, 1986) 96.

f) **A book with a corporate author:** The organization that produced the book (given on the title page) is considered the author.

> 8The Bank of Montreal, <u>The Centenary of the Bank of Montreal, 1817-1917</u> (Montreal: Bank of Montreal, 1917) 42.

> 9Ministry of Colleges and Universities, <u>Horizons: 1989-90 Guide to Postsecondary Education in Ontario</u> (Toronto: Ministry of Education, 1990) 72.

> 10Canadian Historical Association, <u>Regionalism in the Canadian Community, 1867-1967</u>, ed. Mason Wade (Toronto: U of Toronto P, 1969) 221.

g) **A book with no author given:** Do not use Anonymous or Anon. Begin the note with the title (ignoring articles a, an, and the).

> 11<u>1990 Stoddart Restaurant Guide to Toronto</u> (Toronto: Stoddart, 1990) 3.

*Books—Variations in Publication*

h) **An edition other than the first:** An edition is noted by number (e.g., 2nd ed., 3rd ed.), by year (e.g., 1990 ed.), or by name (e.g., Centennial edition, rev. ed.) in keeping with the format of the title page.

> 16T.R.H. Davenport, <u>South Africa: A Modern History</u>, 2nd ed. (Toronto: U of Toronto P, 1978) 100.

i) **A work in several volumes:** Citation format varies depending on the actual reference. If your paper refers to all volumes, the number of the volumes is placed immediately before the publishing information. The specific volume number, denoted by an arabic numeral followed by a colon, will precede the page number(s).

[17]Max Weber, <u>Economy and Society: An Outline of Interpretive Sociology</u>, ed. Guenther Roth and Claus Wittich, trans. Ephraim Fischoff, et al., 3 vols. (New York: Bedminster, 1968) 1: 215-16.

When only one volume is cited, the total number of volumes and the span of publication years may be given at the end of the citation, although the latter is not absolutely necessary. If the volume you have used has a title which is different from the title of the entire collection, give the title of the single volume first. Then, after citing publication details, indicate which volume number you have used, followed by the multivolume title.

[18]Irvin Ehrenpreis, <u>Dean Swift</u> (Cambridge, MA: Harvard UP, 1983) 627-31, vol. 3 of <u>Swift: The Man, His Works, and the Age</u> (Cambridge, MA: Harvard UP, 1969-83).

j) **A book in a series:** The name of the series and the number of the book in that series precede the publication information. The name of the series is neither underlined nor placed in quotation marks.

[19]Nancy Lee Beaty, <u>The Craft of Dying: A Study of the Literary Tradition of the "Ars Moriendi" in England</u>, Yale Studies in English 175 (New Haven, CT: Yale UP, 1970) 54.

k) **A book with a special publisher's imprint:** The name of the special publisher's imprint (in this case Borzoi) is given before the name of the publisher, and both names are joined with a hyphen.

[20]Bruno Bettelheim, <u>The Uses of Enchantment: The Meaning and Importance of Fairy Tales</u> (New York: Borzoi-Knopf, 1976) 235.

l) **A republished book:** When a book has been republished, give the date of the original publication inside the opening parenthesis followed by a semicolon and give the last copyright date (the most recent date of publication) immediately before the closing parenthesis.

> [18]Catharine Parr Traill, <u>Canadian Crusoes: A Tale of the Rice Lake Plains</u> (1852; Ottawa: Carleton UP, 1986) 44.

*Books—Variations in Pagination*

m) **A play that has act, scene, and line numbers:** References to plays follow the same style as books except act, scene, and line numbers are separated by periods, not commas, and there is no need to give a page reference. Some instructors prefer roman to arabic numerals to designate act and scene numbers, e.g., III.ii.73-75, but, for footnotes and endnotes, the more frequently recommended style is to use arabic numerals, e.g., 3.2.73-75. If the author is widely known, as in the case of William Shakespeare, the author's name may be omitted. Because act, scene, and line numbers are the same in all editions of classical works, even the edition and publication data may be omitted if this information is irrelevant to the writer's purpose.

> [19]<u>Hamlet</u>, ed. Edward Hubler (New York: Signet-NAL, 1963) 3.2.73-75.
> or
> [20]<u>Hamlet</u> 3.2.73-75.

Note the absence of a comma after the title.

*Sections of Books*

n) **One part of a book by a single author (e.g., poem, short story, essay, article, or chapter):** The title of the part of the book, placed in quotation marks, comes before the title of the whole book, which is underlined.

> [10]Forrest E. LaViolette, "The Potlatch Law: Wardship and Enforcement," <u>The Struggle for Survival: Indian Cultures and the Protestant Ethic in British Columbia</u> (Toronto: U of Toronto P, 1973) 90.

o) **An article in a book in which there are articles by a number of writers:** The abbreviation "ed." replaces "edited by." The editors' names are placed after the title.

> [11]Kathleen Weiler, "You've Got to Stay There and Fight: Sex Equity, Schooling, and Work," <u>Changing Education: Women as Radicals and Conservators</u>, ed. Joyce Antler and Sari Knopp Bilen (Albany, NY: SUNY P, 1990) 220.

p) **A work in an anthology:** If the work is a short poem, short story, or essay (in other words, a work that has probably not been previously published on its own) enclose the title of this work in quotation marks. If the work is a play, novel, or long poem (in other words, a work that has probably been previously published on its own) underline the title of this work. If your reference is to the anthology as a whole, cite it as an edited text. (See example c.)

> [12]Yeats, W.B., "The Second Coming," <u>The Norton Anthology of English Literature</u>, ed. M.H. Abrams, 5th ed., vol. 2 (New York: Norton, 1986) 1948, lines 22-23.

> [13]Bernard Shaw, <u>Major Barbara, Bernard Shaw's Plays</u>, ed. Warren Sylvester Smith (New York: Norton, 1970) 1-73.

<sup>14</sup>William Shakespeare, <u>Hamlet</u>, <u>William Shakespeare: The Complete Works</u>. ed. Alfred Harbage (Baltimore, MD: Penguin, 1969) 930-76.

Note the page references in the last two examples. In the Shaw example, the entire play can be found on the pages noted. If lines of the play were being referenced, the act, scene, and line or page on which the lines appeared would be referenced. Because this play is not written in verse, either lines or page number may be noted. In the Shakespeare example, the entire play appears on the pages noted and we can assume that the reference is to the entire play. If specific lines were being referenced, act, scene, and line numbers only need be given because this is a play written in verse with numbered lines.

q) **An introduction, preface, foreword, or afterword:** The appropriate label (e.g., Introduction) is given but neither underlined nor put in quotation marks. If the writer of the part being cited differs from the author of the entire work, the word "by" and the author's name follow the title of the work.

<sup>14</sup>Robert Giroux, Introduction, <u>The Complete Stories</u>, by Flannery O'Connor (New York: Farrar, 1971) xv.

r) **An article in a reference book (encyclopaedia, dictionary):** If the article has an author, begin with that author's name in normal order. (Remember that in reference books, authorship is often indicated only by initials, usually given at the close of an article. If the author's name is abbreviated to initials, find the key to abbreviations or the list of contributing authors, and give the author's full name in your citation.) If there is no author indicated, begin with the title of the article. You may omit page and volume number when articles appear alphabetically in the source. Only the year of publication need be given for well-known multivolume reference books.

<sup>15</sup>Julia Cairns, "Spry, Constance," <u>Dictionary of National Biography 1951-1960</u>, 1971 ed., 915.

<sup>16</sup>"Axminster Carpets," <u>Encyclopaedia Britannica: Micropaedia</u>, 1974.

**First References to Articles in Periodicals: Guidelines and Examples**

An entry for an article in a periodical (journal, magazine, or newspaper), like an entry for a book, must include all the information necessary for your reader to find the item you have cited. When articles from periodicals are cited, information in the first footnote or endnote is usually arranged in the following order.

1. Author's name, first name followed by last name
2. Title of the article, in quotation marks
3. Name of the periodical, underlined
4. Publication data—Series number or name
     —Volume number, in arabic
     —Issue number
     —Publication date (in parentheses for journals, but
     without parentheses for magazines and newspapers)
5. Page number(s)

Items in a note are generally separated by a comma and all numbers are generally recorded in arabic numerals.

How this information is arranged and punctuated, and what information is actually included, depend to a large extent on the type of periodical being noted. For example, in a footnote referring to an article in a magazine, you do not list the volume and issue number, but you do list the complete date of publication, including the day. Pay close attention to the variations in the following examples to determine what to note, how to order information, and how to punctuate entries. Where no specific example is given (e.g., for notes on works by multiple authors), follow the general guidelines given for books.

a) **Journal articles: An article published in a journal with continuous pagination throughout the annual volume:** The volume number (83), but not the issue number, is given.

 [1]David E. Bynum, "Themes of the Young Hero in Serbocroatian Oral Epic Tradition," <u>PMLA</u> 83 (1968): 1296.

**An article from a journal that paginates each issue separately:** The volume number (19) and the issue number (4) are both given since each of the four issues of volume 19 could have a page 55.

²Edgar J. Dosman, "Hemispheric Relations in the 1980s: A Perspective from Canada," <u>Journal of Canadian Studies</u> 19.4 (1984): 55.

b) **Magazine articles:** In a note for an article from a weekly or biweekly magazine, the complete date (including the day) is given in place of volume and issue numbers. If the magazine is published monthly, the month may be listed without the day. The names of all months are abbreviated with the exceptions of May, June, and July.

³Harvey Wheeler, "The Politics of Ecology," <u>Saturday Review</u> 7 Mar. 1970: 52.

c) **Newspaper articles:** If the name of a newspaper on the masthead begins with an introductory article, give the name of the newspaper but omit the article, e.g., <u>Globe and Mail</u>, not <u>The Globe and Mail</u>. When the place of publication is not part of the newspaper's title, it is added in square brackets after the title. When the newspaper has different editions, the name of the edition that appears on the masthead is placed after the date and preceded by a comma. When each section is paginated separately, the appropriate section letter and the page number are given.

⁴Brian Milner, "GATT Decries Growing Wave of Protectionism," <u>Globe and Mail</u> [Toronto] 28 Mar. 1985, Metro ed.: B3.

If the name of the author is not given, begin with the title of the article.

⁵"Ottawa Cuts Crimp Science, Tech Data," <u>Globe and Mail</u> [Toronto] 14 May 1992, Metro ed.: B4.

d) **Letter to an editor or an editorial:** If the letter or editorial is untitled, the appropriate label, neither underlined nor in quotation marks, is given after the name of the author.

> ⁶Ravi Baichwal, letter, <u>Saturday Night</u> July-Aug. 1990: 8.

If the submission is titled, the label is given after the title, which is enclosed in quotation marks.

> ⁷Lewis Lapham, "Achievement Test," editorial, <u>Harper's</u> July 1991: 13.

e) **Review (of a book, movie, or live performance):** For a book review, the name of the reviewer, first name followed by last name, is followed by the title of the review in quotation marks, then "rev. of ," the name of the book underlined, the name of the author of the book, the periodical information, and finally, the page number(s). If the review has no title, place "rev. of" immediately after the name of the reviewer.

> ⁸John Fowles, "Literature's Good Soldier," rev. of <u>Ford Madox Ford</u> by Alan Judd, <u>Atlantic</u> May 1991: 114.

For a performance review, add the relevant production information, such as place of performance and name of performing company:

> ⁹Edith Oliver, "Antic Dane," rev. of <u>Hamlet</u> by William Shakespeare, Roundabout Theatre Company, Criterion Centre, New York, <u>New Yorker</u> 13 Apr. 1992: 82.

### References to Other Sources: Guidelines and Examples

Notes on other sources such as films, lectures, interviews, and computer software follow the same general pattern as notes on books and published articles.

**Print Material**

a) **Government documents:** When no author is given, the government body is treated as the author. The name of the government author is followed by the title of the document, underlined. When title pages are given in more than one language, only one version need be used. After the title, the available relevant publication information is given (publisher, place and date of publication, pages, etc.). Citing government documents can be complicated, but the Government Documents librarian or another member of the library staff will be able to help you.

[1]Ontario Legislative Assembly, Standing Committee on Social Development, <u>Report on Food Banks</u>, 2nd session, 34th Parliament (Toronto: Government of Ontario, April 1990) 21-22.

[2]Ontario Legislative Assembly, Standing Committee on Social Development, <u>Debates</u>, 3rd session, 32nd Parliament (Toronto: Government of Ontario, May 1983) S-6.

b) **Dissertations or theses**

**Unpublished:** The title is placed in quotation marks, not underlined. The title is followed by a designation such as "diss." or "M.A. thesis," the name of the university where the dissertation or thesis was submitted, and the year of its completion.

[16]Christine Niero, "Making Stories: Studies in Contemporary Canadian Metafiction," diss., Queen's U, 1987, 2.

**Published:** The title is underlined, the name of the university and the date of completion are given, and the publication information, including the order number, follows.

[17]A.G. Finley, Shipbuilding in St. Martins 1840-1880: A Case Study of Family Enterprise on the Fundy Shore, M.A. thesis, U of New Brunswick 1980 (Ottawa: Canadian Theses on Microfiche, 1984) 47732, 18.

c) **Pamphlets:** In general, treat a pamphlet as you would a book. If there is no author, cite the name of the pamphlet first. Often, publication details will be sketchy: use n.p. for "no known publisher," N.p. for "no known place of publication," N. pag. for "no pagination," and n.d. for "no date given" to indicate missing data.

[19]Human Rights: What to Do about Discrimination or Harassment (Peterborough, ON: Trent U, n.d.) n. pag.

d) **Archival material:**  The format for citing archival material varies; however, certain pieces of standard information are necessary in all archival citations. The citation must first allow the reader to locate the archival material by identifying the repository and the material's location within the repository; it must also describe the material as any citation would, giving author, date, etc. For more information consult Terry Cook, ed., Archival Citations: Suggestions for the Citation of Documents at the Public Archives of Canada (Ottawa: Public Archives, 1983). The Public Archives of Canada is now called the National Archives of Canada, and abbreviated NAC as in the sample entry below. RG stands for Record Group (the collection in the NAC where the material may be found). The material cited here can be located on pages 131 and 132 of volume 1846.

[18]NAC RG10, vol. 1846, 131, 132, "Treaty No. 3 between Her Majesty the Queen and the Saulteaux Tribe of the Ojibbeway Indians at the Northwest Angle of the Lake of the Woods with Adhesions, 3 October 1873."

e) **Legal documents/court cases:** A good standard source for the conventions for citing legal documents is the <u>Canadian Guide to Uniform Legal Citation</u> (Toronto: Carswell, 1992) which provides information on documenting statutes, bills, by-laws, regulations, codes, cases, treaties, and international agreements. In general, a citation of a legal document must include the following: identification of case or document, date of document, and information making clear where the document can be found (name, volume, and page of court report, for example).

f) **Material from an information service:** Cite the material from the service much the same way you would cite other printed material, giving publication information. Add the name of the service and the file number at the end of the entry. If the material has not been published previously, cite the service as the publisher. No place of publication is needed. Retain the file number at the end of the citation.

[15]Liddy Limbrick, et al., <u>Peer-Power: Using Peer Tutoring to Help Low-Progress Readers in Primary and Secondary Schools</u> (Wellington: New Zealand Council for Educational Research, 1985) 10 (ERIC ED 326 858).

[16]Susan B. Thomas, "Concerns about Gifted Children: A Paper and Abstract Bibliography" (ERIC: 1974) 23 (ERIC ED 091 083).

## Non-print Material

a) **Lectures, addresses, debates:** Following the speaker's name and the title of the lecture, give the name of the course, meeting, or sponsor, the location, and the date. If the title of the presentation is not known, use an accurate descriptive word (e.g., Lecture, Address, Debate). Do not underline this word or place it in quotation marks.

[9]John Syrett, "Nixon the Great Before Watergate," Hist. 312, Trent U, 7 Mar. 1984.

b) **Personal communications (interviews, letters):** Give the name of the person approached, the appropriate descriptive label (e.g., Personal Interview, Telephone Interview, Personal Letter), and the date.

> ¹⁰Judith A. O'Donoghue, Personal Interview, 9 Apr. 1985.

c) **Works of art:** When the work of art has been reproduced in a book, reference the work as you would a section of a book:

> ⁶Michelangelo, <u>The Rondanini Pieta</u>, Museo del Castello Sforzesco, Milan, plate 38 in <u>Testament: The Bible as History</u>, by John Romer (New York: Holt, 1988) 326.

When the work of art is viewed in its original form or found in an unpublished source, give the artist's name, the name of the work underlined, the name of the institution housing the artwork, and the location. The location may be cited by city or by city and country (when the city is not widely known).

> ⁷Rosa Bonheur, <u>Plowing Scene</u>, Museum of Fine Arts, Boston.

d) **Films, television and radio programs, slide programs and video-tapes, and sound recordings:** Unlike books and articles where the author is almost always the creator of what is being cited, in documents such as films, TV programs, and records, many people contribute to the end product. In general, the information most relevant to your textual reference is given first (the name of the film or the song, the director or the producer of a performance, etc.). In addition, your reader will need to know the name of the document, the production information, and the year of production.

**Film—reference to film content**

> ¹<u>PowWow at Duck Lake</u>, prod. John Kemeny and Barrie Howells, dir. Bonnie Klein, NFB, 1968.

### Film—reference to director

[2]Peter Watkins, writer and dir., <u>The War Game</u>,
BBC, 1966.

### Television program—reference to program

[3]"Land of the Eagle," <u>Nature</u>, PBS, WNED, Buffalo,
NY, 3 May 1992.

### Television program—reference to actor

[4]Tony Danza, actor, <u>Growing Pains</u>, ABC, CHEX,
Peterborough, ON, 25 Apr. 1992.

### Sound recording—reference to lyrics

[4]David Byrne, "The Big Country," <u>The Talking
Heads: More Songs about Buildings and Food</u>, Sire,
9147-6058, 1978.

Note that in the preceding example David Byrne wrote the lyrics.

### Sound recording—reference to producer

[23]Phil Spector, prod., <u>Let It Be</u>, The Beatles,
Apple, SW-6386, 1970.

### Video-tape—reference to video-tape content

[5]<u>Science Study Skills, Section Two: Science Labs</u>,
video-tape, prod. Ann Wetmore and Christine Shelton,
Mount Saint Vincent University Student Affairs Dept.,
1991.

e) **Live performance:** Guidelines for performances are much the same as those for films. Rather than giving the year of release, cite the theatre, city, and date of performance.

[8]<u>Counsellors-at-Law</u>, by Elmer Rice, dir. Neil
Munro, with James Mezon, Shaw Festival, Niagara-on-
the-Lake, 29 May 1992.

f) **Computer software:** Since the authors of most software are not named, the title of the software, underlined, is usually written first. However, if the author's name is known, it should be placed, in normal order, before the title of the program. Follow the title with the version, preceded by the abbreviation "vers." and the label "computer software." Complete the note with the name of the supplier, followed by a comma and the year of issue or copyright.

[11]<u>Wordstar</u>, computer software, Micropro International, 1983.

[12]Dan Bricklin and Bob Frankston, <u>VisiCalc</u>, computer software, Software Arts, Apr. 1979.

If the program has been designed under contract to a major computer firm for which the program has been designed (e.g., IBM or Apple), add this information after the date, and give the edition number if known. Also add, if known, the number of kilobytes (e.g., 64KB), the operating system (e.g., IBM PC-DOS 2.10), and the form of the program (cartridge, cassette, or, more commonly, disk). Separate each of these items with a comma and put a period at the end:

[13]<u>Microsoft Disk Operating System</u>, computer software, Microsoft Corp., Sept. 1983, IBM, IBM PC-DOS 2.10, disk.

Note that sometimes you will find that where a major computer company owns the program, the company's name is listed first:

[14]Tandy, <u>Studymate: The Grade Booster</u>, vers. 2.1, computer software, Compu-Teach Corp., 1990, IBM PC, disk.

### Citing an Indirect Source in an Endnote or Footnote

When citing an indirect source, that is, when citing the work of an author as it is found in the work of another author, cite both the primary source (the work cited) and the secondary source (the work in which you found the material). Write "qtd. in" before giving the reference for the secondary source. For instance, you might write the following:

> As J.B. Priestley, the author who became one of
> Britain's favourite broadcasters during World War
> II, writes, "I had no direct evidence but I soon
> came to believe—and friends more in the know than
> I was agreed with me—that it was Churchill who had
> me taken off the air."[33]

Your footnote would then look like this:

> [33]J.B. Priestley, <u>All England Listened</u> (New
> York, 1967) xx, qtd. in Joseph P. Lash, <u>Roosevelt</u>
> <u>and Churchill, 1939-1941: The Partnership That</u>
> <u>Saved the West </u>(New York: Norton, 1976) 278.

If the publication data is not available for the original source, give the author's name only, followed by "qtd. in."

> [33]J.B. Priestley, qtd. in Joseph P. Lash,
> <u>Roosevelt and Churchill, 1939-1941: The Partnership</u>
> <u>that Saved the West</u> (New York: Norton, 1976) 278.

## VARIATION OF STANDARD FORM

When you are citing one source frequently in your essay, subsequent references to it may be made in the body of the essay simply by giving the relevant page numbers in parentheses. For example, the first footnote to a single work upon which an essay is based can indicate to the reader that all further references to that work will appear by page number (when referring to prose), by line number (when referring to poetry), or by act, scene, and line number (when referring to drama) in parentheses throughout the text.

The first footnote to the source has full bibliographical information followed by a line such as "All further references to this work will be from this edition and will be parenthetically noted by (page; line; page and line; act, scene, and line) number(s) throughout the text of this essay," or, for example, a note might read:

> [4]Unless otherwise stated, all references to the prefaces of the novels of Henry James are taken from Henry James, The Art of the Novel: Critical Prefaces (New York: Scribner's, 1962).

A subsequent in-text reference might read:

> James compares life with the art of the novelist: "life being all inclusion and confusion, and art being all discrimination and selection, the latter, in search of the hard latent value with which alone it is concerned, sniffs around the mass as instinctively and unerringly as a dog suspicious of some buried bone" (120).

More than one major source of a paper can be documented in this way. Most often when the essay compares two or more novels, two or more critics, or two or more theorists, the parenthetical reference will contain a surname and the appropriate number(s). The writer must make certain that the first footnote makes the in-text referencing clear and that the parenthetical references do not create any confusion or undue textual clutter. In this method of documentation, in-text references should be kept, as much as possible, to numbers only, to a name and appropriate number(s), or to a single word designation or an abbreviation of a title and the appropriate number(s). For example, the first note might read:

> [1]Northrop Frye's works are referenced in the text of this paper by page number and by the following initials for titles:
> MC: The Modern Century (Toronto: Oxford UP, 1967)
> AC: Anatomy of Criticism: Four Essays (Princeton: Princeton UP, 1957)

An excerpt from the text might read:

> In 1967, Frye referred to modern social mythology as a "faint parody of the Christian mythology that preceded it" (MC 111). Earlier, he had developed the full range of his theory of myths, including Christian myths, within the context of literary criticism (AC 131-239).

Including short parenthetical documentation in the text avoids the nuisance of having to create a long list of notes containing nothing more than a page number, or a repeated abbreviation and page number. It was once common to use Latin abbreviations in second and subsequent references. Although you should be aware of the meanings of these abbreviations because you may encounter them in your readings, they are seldom , if ever, used in essays today. "Op. cit." (opere citato) means "in the work cited" and refers to a different page of a work recently cited. "Loc. cit." (loco citato) means "in the place cited" and refers to the same passage cited in a recent note. "Ibid." (ibidem) means "in the same place" and is used only when the reference is to the work in the footnote immediately preceding it.

**Supplementary Footnotes**

Footnotes, besides giving documentation, can also provide information which cannot be easily incorporated into your text. Supplementary footnotes usually define, amplify, or qualify material you are discussing, or they refer the reader to other sources. They can be used with both the **parenthetical** and **footnoting** methods of documentation.

> [38]These conclusions have also been reached by L. Baird, "Big School, Small School: A Critical Examination of the Hypothesis," Journal of Educational Psychology 60 (1969): 253-60.

Note that full bibliographical information for the source of this additional information has been (and should be) included.

Supplementary notes can also invite the reader to investigate the sources that provide contextual information. The writer asks the reader to "see ...," or uses the letters "cf" (which means "to compare") to invite the reader to compare information in the text with the information given in other sources. These notes are often called **cross-references**. For example, a cross-reference might read:

> [2]Dorothy Livesay, "Day and Night," <u>Horizon: Writings of the Canadian Prairie</u>, ed. Ken Mitchell (Toronto: Oxford UP, 1977) 112-15. For comparison, see Livesay's later love poems in Dorothy Livesay, <u>The Woman I Am</u> (Don Mills, ON: Musson, 1977) and Dorothy Livesay, <u>The Phases of Love</u> (Toronto: Coach House, 1983).

Although supplementary footnotes are useful in that they allow the writer the flexibility to include additional information, you should remember that the primary purpose of footnotes is to document the sources of cited material. Therefore, the notes should not contain extraneous and discursive exposition. The writer should consider the information given in each note carefully: if a note contains significant substantive material, it is often better to incorporate that information into the body of the paper; if information is pertinent but too lengthy and detailed to footnote, you may decide to add it as an appendix.

# PARENTHETICAL DOCUMENTATION:
# STYLE A (MLA STYLE)

As has been noted, the method of parenthetical documentation called Style A in this handbook is based on the guidelines set by the Modern Language Association (MLA). Its chief distinction is that it usually requires no more than the author's name and the page reference in the parenthetical reference: (author page). Style A is most commonly used in the humanities, especially in disciplines such as English literature and philosophy, subjects in which the date of publication of an article or book is not usually central to the argument being made. It is also the preferred form for interdisciplinary essays where the nature of the focus is close to philosophy or English literature (in women's studies or native studies for example).

## THE STANDARD PARENTHETICAL REFERENCE
## IN THE ESSAY

Whenever an idea, piece of information, or quotation from one of your sources appears in the essay, a parenthetical reference, including the author's last name and the relevant page number(s), is inserted next to the borrowed item. The author's name enables your readers to identify the source in the list of works cited, and the page number tells them exactly where the material can be found:

```
Policy during the Milner era denied the Africans,
Asians, and coloured people access to full
citizenship (Davenport 152).
```

This statement about the policy of the Milner era appears on page 152 of the work by Davenport listed in "Works Cited." Note that the reference does not contain any punctuation or abbreviation for the word "page" or "pages." The author's name and the page number are separated by a single space.

See page 84(i) for the corresponding entry as it would appear in "Works Cited."

The format for citing articles is the same as the format for citing books. To cite a single article by a single author, give the author's surname and the relevant page number. For example, write (Bynum 1298) to cite something on page 1298 of the article "Themes of the Young Hero in Serbocroatian Oral Epic Tradition." See page 88(a) for the corresponding entry as it would appear in "Works Cited."

### Position and Punctuation of the Parenthetical Citation

The parenthetical reference should be placed close to the material it documents, preferably at the end of a sentence. When the material being documented is not a block quotation, the reference is usually given before the concluding punctuation mark and, where there is one, after the closing quotation mark:

```
The missionaries, unlike the fur traders, subjected
the natives to "an institutionalized mode of
cultural dismemberment and reconstruction"
(LaViolette 18).
```

See page 85(n) for the corresponding entry as it would appear in "Works Cited."

Sometimes it is not possible to place a reference at the end of a sentence without confusing the reader about what is being documented. If the reference must be placed mid-sentence, position the citation as closely as possible to the material being cited, preferably at a natural pause in the sentence.

```
One historian refers to "cultural dismemberment"
(LaViolette 18), while others use the term
"assimilation" (Tobias 39).
```

To document a block quotation, first give the concluding punctuation of the quotation; then leave two spaces and insert the parenthetical reference:

The European colonials sought to enforce systematically the acculturation of the natives:

> The casualness of the fur trading type of contacts could no longer be tolerated. Hence, with the arrival of the missionaries and  their Christian ethic the task of converting the natives began, and peaceful penetration entered a new phase, based upon an institutionalized mode of cultural dismemberment and reconstruction. (LaViolette 18)

Note the difference here in closing punctuation. The parenthetical reference does not need to be enclosed within a sentence.

## VARIATIONS ON THE STANDARD PARENTHETICAL CITATION

### Avoiding Redundancy
In the examples above, the standard form has been demonstrated: (author page). In most cases, it is the form required. However, parenthetical references should be as concise as possible so, if the information contained in your reference is clear from the text, the parenthetical reference can be modified.

For instance, you need not include the author's name in a parenthetical reference if the name appears in the sentence preceding the parenthetical citation.

*Author's Name in Text*

> Brody draws attention to the emphasis on naming in the language of the Inummariit (134-35).

See page 82(a) for the corresponding entry as it would appear in "Works Cited."

If you are citing an idea that runs through an entire work by an author whose name you have given in the text, you need not include a parenthetical reference at all. Provided that there is only one text by the author in your list of works cited, the author's name is the only documentation required:

> Weiler makes the case that sex equity is a complex goal.

See page 86(o) for the corresponding entry as it would appear in "Works Cited."

Moreover, if your essay makes reference to only one text and author (as is the case with many introductory literature and philosophy essays, for example), you may need to give the author's name only in the first parenthetical citation. It will be clear to the reader that the other references, which will consist only of page numbers, are to the same text.

### Citing One of Two or More Works by the Same Author

Sometimes the author's last name alone will not direct your reader to the correct corresponding entry. If, for example, you have referred to more than one work by the same author, you must include in your reference a shortened version of the title of the relevant work after the author's name. Note that a comma is used to separate the author's name and the title:

> Milton's prose has been described as "controlled personal feeling expressed through deliberate rhetorical devices" (Daiches, <u>Milton</u> 103).

The inclusion of the title allows the reader to decide to which of the works by Daiches listed in "Works Cited" you are referring. See page 82(b) for the corresponding entry as it would appear in "Works Cited."

## Citing Works by More than One Author

If a work cited has more than one author, references to it must include all the authors' surnames or the first author's surname followed by "et al.," paralleling the format used for the entry in the list of works cited:

The war in Vietnam overshadowed the struggle in Laos (Langer and Zasloff 1).

Some researchers believe that girls go through stages of intellectual development different from those of boys (Belenky et al. 42-64).

See pages 83(e) and 83(f) for the corresponding entries as they would appear in "Works Cited."

## Citing a Work Listed by Title

If a work is listed by title in "Works Cited," give the title or a shortened version of it in the parenthetical citation:

A recent article in the Globe and Mail notes that budget cuts to Statistics Canada will result in fewer facts about science and technology being available to Canadians ("Ottawa Cuts" B4).

See page 89(c) for the corresponding entry as it would appear in "Works Cited."

## Citing Location of Material (Other Than by Page Number)

*Multivolume Works*

A page number alone will not always identify the location of a source as specifically as necessary. A reference to a multivolume work must also include the relevant volume number. After the author's name give the volume number, a colon, a space, and the page reference.

For example, a reference to material on page 141 of volume 3 of Economy and Society: An Outline of Interpretive Sociology, written by Max Weber, would be given as (Weber 3: 141).

See page 84(j) for the corresponding entry as it would appear in "Works Cited."

*Works of Literature*

In references to works of literature, it is often preferable to specify location by some designation other than page number—for example, canto, stanza, book, or act, scene, and line. Use periods to separate the numbers in the reference, and avoid abbreviations except when they are necessary to establish what the numbers designate:

```
                        Give me that man
    That is not passion's slave, and I will wear him
    In my heart's core, ay, in my heart of heart …
    (3.2.73-75)
```

Here the reference indicates that the passage quoted appears in act 3, scene 2, lines 73-75 of the edition of <u>Hamlet</u> listed in "Works Cited." (Note that some instructors prefer Roman to Arabic numerals to designate act and scene, e.g., III.ii.73-75.) See page 86(p) for the corresponding entry as it would appear in "Works Cited."

*Documenting Sources Cited by Other Sources*

When possible, take material from its original source. However, it is sometimes necessary to cite a source indirectly—that is, to cite a quotation, not from where it was originally written, but from a text in which it is quoted. To document such sources, write "qtd. in" (quoted in) before giving the reference for the secondary source:

```
    Teresa deLauretis notes that micropolitical groups
    can have an impact through "shifting the 'ground'
    of a given sign" (qtd. in Weiler 218).
```

See page 86(o) for the corresponding entry as it would appear in "Works Cited."

## The List of Works Cited

Any essay using parenthetical documentation Style A must be accompanied by a list of works cited, usually titled "Works Cited," so that the reader may have full publication information for all parenthetical references. Each parenthetical reference, therefore, must have a corresponding entry in "Works Cited." Moreover, no texts should be listed in "Works Cited" to which no reference is made in the essay.

Because the format and conventions of the list of works cited are identical to those for the footnoting method of documentation, the student should follow the guidelines on pages 80, 81 to prepare a list of works cited to accompany a paper using parenthetical documentation Style A.

# BIBLIOGRAPHY OR WORKS CITED
# (FOR FOOTNOTING AND STYLE A)

In the footnoting system of documentation, the notes are normally accompanied by a bibliography, titled "Bibliography."[1] In parenthetical documentation Style A, the parenthetical references are accompanied by a list of works cited, that is, a list of every work to which there is a parenthetical reference in the text of the essay.

The only visible difference between the bibliography that usually accompanies a footnoted essay and the list of works cited that accompanies an essay using parenthetical documentation Style A is the title. Conventions for arrangement and punctuation of entries are identical. However, there is an important conceptual difference between a bibliography and a list of works cited. The word "bibliography" usually indicates a complete list of all the works consulted during the research of an essay, even those to which no reference is made in the essay. Works cited means precisely what it says; only works to which there is direct reference in the essay are listed. Works that have been consulted but not cited are not included in a list of works cited.

Because the format for entries in a bibliography is identical to that of a list of works cited, this format will be described in detail only once in this text, in the section that follows.

### Arrangement of Entries:

—Entries are arranged alphabetically by author's last name on a separate page entitled "Works Cited" or "Bibliography," whichever is accurate, at the end of the essay.

—The page, or pages if the list requires more than one sheet, should be numbered in sequence with the pages of the essay.

---

[1] Occasionally, it may not be necessary for a student using the footnoting method to compile a bibliography, especially if an essay refers to only one text and the publication information for that text is clear from the footnote. Instructors will specify when a bibliography is unnecessary; unless your instructor has indicated otherwise, include a bibliography in a footnoted essay.

Another corollary: in some disciplines using the footnoting method, a list of only those works which have been cited in the text of the essay is required. If this is the format your instructor requests, title the list "Works Cited" or "References."

—The first line of each entry begins flush with the left margin, and subsequent lines are indented five spaces.

—Double-spacing is used between entries, and single-spacing or double-spacing within entries.

## Entries for Books and Sections of Books: Guidelines

In general, an entry must contain information about author, title, and publication data. For a typical text with one author and the usual publishing information, the entry is relatively straightforward. Furthermore, if the text you are citing conforms exactly to one of our examples, you can follow the conventions of the example.

However, some of your citations may not conform precisely to one of the examples given. For example, you may want to cite a text that is translated, that is a second edition, and that is part of a multi-volume work. Although Notes provides guidelines for each of these variations individually, there is not sufficient space to describe all possible combinations. For that reason, provided below is a guide to the order in which various elements of information should be presented.

Begin a complex citation by using the example that most closely describes what you are citing. To place information not displayed in the example, follow the order given below. Following these steps should allow you to master any combination of documentation data.

Information for books or sections of books, then, is normally arranged in the following order:

1. Author's name, last name first
2. Title of the part of the book used (e.g., article within book, poem)
3. Title of the book, as it appears on the title page
4. Name of the editor or translator
5. Edition, if other than first
6. Volume number(s)
7. Series name
8. Place of publication
9. Publisher's name
10. Date of publication
11. Page number(s)

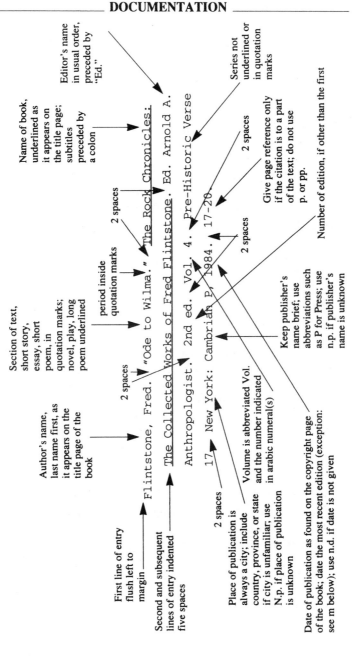

This information should be arranged and punctuated in accordance with the following example:

Editor's name in usual order, preceded by "Ed."

Name of book, underlined as it appears on the title page; subtitles preceded by a colon

Series not underlined or in quotation marks

Section of text, short story, essay, short poem, in quotation marks; novel, play, long poem underlined

2 spaces

period inside quotation marks

Give page reference only if the citation is to a part of the text; do not use p. or pp.

Author's name, last name first, as it appears on the title page of the book

2 spaces

Number of edition, if other than the first

Keep publisher's name brief; use abbreviations such as P for Press; use n.p. if publisher's name is unknown

2 spaces

Flintstone, Fred. "Ode to Wilma." The Rock Chronicles: The Collected Works of Fred Flintstone. Ed. Arnold A. Anthropologist. 2nd ed. Vol. 4. Pre-Historic Verse 17 New York: Cambrian P, 1984. 17-20.

First line of entry flush left to margin

Second and subsequent lines of entry indented five spaces

Volume is abbreviated Vol. and the number indicated in arabic numeral(s)

2 spaces

Place of publication is always a city; include country, province, or state if city is unfamiliar; use N.p. if place of publication is unknown

Date of publication as found on the copyright page of the book; date the most recent edition (exception: see m below); use n.d. if date is not given

81

This diagram provides general information. For details about citing a specific type of source, consult the examples that follow.

## Entries for Published Books and Sections of Books: Examples

*Books—Variations of Author*

a) **A book with a single author:**

Brody, Hugh. <u>The People's Land: Eskimos and Whites in the Eastern Arctic.</u> Harmondsworth, Eng.: Penguin, 1975.

b) **Two or more works by the same author:** The author's name is given in the first entry only. In additional entries it is replaced by three unspaced hyphens and a period.

Daiches, David. <u>Critical Approaches to Literature</u>. Englewood Cliffs, NJ: Prentice-Hall, 1956.

—. <u>Milton</u>. New York: Norton Library—Norton, 1966.

c) **A book with a single author and an editor or translator, when references are to the author, not the editor:** The editor's name, preceded by Ed. (or the translator's name, preceded by Trans.) is given after the title. If a book has both a translator and an editor, list the names as they appear on the book's title page.

Dickens, Charles. <u>The Personal History of David Copperfield</u>. Ed. Trevor Blount. Harmondsworth, Eng.: Penguin, 1966.

d) **A book with an editor or translator, when references are to the edited material: the introduction, notes, editorial decisions regarding layout, etc.:**

Olling, R.D., and M.W. Westmacott, eds. <u>The Confederation Debate: The Constitution in Crisis</u>. Toronto: Kendall/Hunt, 1980.

e) **A book with either two or three authors:** The first author's name is given surname first to facilitate alphabetical listing. All other names are given in their normal order.

Langer, Paul F., and Joseph Zasloff. North Vietnam and the Pathet Lao: Partners in the Struggle for Laos. Cambridge, MA: Harvard UP, 1970.

f) **A book with more than three authors:** Information can be cited in two ways. Either the first author only, followed by "et al." ("and others"), is given, or all authors' names are given, presented in the order that they appear on the book's title page. Normally, if "et al." is used in the parenthetical citation or footnote, the names of all authors are given in the works cited or bibliographic entry.

Belenky, Mary Field, et al. Women's Ways of Knowing: The Development of Self, Voice, and Mind. New York: Basic, 1986.

Belenky, Mary Field, Blythe McVicker Clinchy, Nancy Rule Goldberg, and Jill Mattuck Tarule. Women's Ways of Knowing: The Development of Self, Voice, and Mind. New York: Basic, 1986.

g) **A book with a corporate author:** The organization that produced the book (given on the title page) is considered the author.

Bank of Montreal. The Centenary of the Bank of Montreal, 1817-1917. Montreal: Bank of Montreal, 1917.

Ministry of Colleges and Universities. Horizons: 1989-1990 Guide to Postsecondary Education in Ontario. Toronto: Ministry of Education, 1990.

Canadian Historical Association. Regionalism in the Canadian Community 1867-1967. Ed. Mason Wade. Toronto: U of Toronto P, 1969.

h) **A book with no author given:** Do not use Anonymous or Anon. Begin the entry with the title and alphabetize it according to the first word in the title (ignoring articles a, an, and the). If the first word is a number, as in the example below, alphabetize according to the letter with which the number begins (N for nineteen-ninety).

```
1990 Stoddart Restaurant Guide to Toronto. Toronto:
    Stoddart, 1990.
```

*Books—Variations in Publication*

i) **An edition other than the first:** An edition is noted by number (e.g., 2nd ed., 3rd ed.), year (e.g., 1990 ed.) or by name (e.g., Centennial ed., Rev. ed) in keeping with the format used on the title page.

```
Davenport, T.R.H. South Africa: A Modern History.  2nd
    ed.  Toronto: U of Toronto P, 1978.
```

j) **A work in several volumes:** Citation method varies depending on actual reference. If reference is to all volumes, the number of volumes is placed immediately before the publishing information.

```
Weber, Max. Economy and Society: An Outline of
    Interpretive Sociology.  Ed. Guenther Roth and
    Claus Wittich.  Trans. Ephraim Fischoff, et al.  3
    vols. New York: Bedminster, 1968.
```

When only one volume is cited, the number of volumes and the span of publication years may be given at the end of the citation, although this is not absolutely necessary. If the volume used has a title which is different from the title of the entire collection, give the title of the single volume first. Then, after citing publication details, provide the number of the volume used and the overall title.

```
Ehrenpreis, Irvin. Dean Swift.  Cambridge, MA:
    Harvard UP, 1983.  Vol. 3 of Swift: The Man, His
    Works, and the Age.  3 vols. 1969-83.
```

k) **A book in a series:** The name of the series and the number of the book in that series precede the publication information. The series name is neither underlined nor placed in quotation marks.

Beaty, Nancy Lee. <u>The Craft of Dying: A Study of the Literary Tradition of the "Ars Moriendi" in England</u>. Yale Studies in English 175. New Haven, CT: Yale UP, 1970.

l) **A book with a special publisher's imprint:** The name of the special publisher's imprint (in this case Borzoi) is given before the name of the publisher, and both names are joined with a hyphen.

Bettelheim, Bruno. <u>The Uses of Enchantment: The Meaning and Importance of Fairy Tales</u>. New York: Borzoi-Knopf, 1976.

m) **A republished book:** Sometimes you may wish to make clear to your reader that the publication date of a text you are using is not the date it was first published. When you wish to draw attention to the fact that a book has been republished, give the date of the original publication before the most recent publishing information.

Traill, Catharine Parr. <u>Canadian Crusoes: A Tale of the Rice Lake Plains</u>. 1852. Ottawa: Carleton UP, 1986.

*Sections of Books*

n) **One part of a book by a single author (e.g., essay, short story, poem, article, or chapter):**

LaViolette, Forrest E. "The Potlatch Law: Wardship and Enforcement." <u>The Struggle for Survival: Indian Cultures and the Protestant Ethic in British Columbia</u>. Toronto: U of Toronto P, 1973. 44-97.

o) **An article in a book in which there are articles by a number of writers:**

Weiler, Kathleen. "You've Got to Stay There and Fight:
Sex Equity, Schooling, and Work." <u>Changing
Education: Women as Radicals and Conservators</u>.
Ed. Joyce Antler and Sari Knopp Bilen. Albany, NY:
SUNY P, 1990. 217-36.

p) **A work in an anthology:** If the work is a short poem, short story, or essay (in other words, a work that has probably not been previously published on its own), enclose it in quotation marks. If the work is a long poem, play, or novel (in other words, a work that has probably been previously published on its own), underline the title of the work. If your reference is to the anthology as a whole, cite it as an edited text. (See example d.)

Yeats, W.B. "The Second Coming." <u>The Norton
Anthology of English Literature</u>. Ed. M.H. Abrams.
5th ed. Vol. 2. New York: Norton, 1986. 1948.

Shaw, Bernard. <u>Major Barbara. Bernard Shaw's Plays</u>.
Ed. Warren Sylvester Smith. New York: Norton, 1970.
1-73.

Shakespeare, William. <u>Hamlet. William Shakespeare: The
Complete Works.</u> Ed. Alfred Harbage. Baltimore, MD:
Penguin, 1969. 930-76.

q) **An introduction, preface, foreword, or afterword:** The appropriate label (e.g., Introduction) is given, but it is neither underlined nor placed in quotation marks. If the writer of the part being cited differs from the author of the entire work, the word "By" and the author's name follow the title of the work.

Giroux, Robert. Introduction. <u>The Complete Stories</u>.
By Flannery O'Connor. New York: Farrar, 1971.
vii-xvii.

r) **An article in a reference book (encyclopaedia, dictionary):** In general, treat the reference as you would an article in a book. If there is no author, begin with the title of the article. (Remember that in encyclopaedias, often only the author's initials are given at the close of the article. You will need to locate the reference guide which provides the author's full name.) If articles are arranged alphabetically in the reference book, do not include page or volume numbers. For familiar publications such as the Encyclopaedia Britannica, full publication data need not be given—just cite the year of publication.

Cairns, Julia. "Spry, Constance." Dictionary of
    National Biography 1951-1960.  1971 ed.

"Axminster Carpets." Encyclopaedia Britannica:
    Micropaedia. 1974.

### Entries for Articles in Periodicals: Guidelines

An entry for an article, like an entry for a book, must include all the information necessary for your reader to find the item you have cited. When articles from periodicals are cited, information is normally arranged in the following order.

1. Author's name, last name first
2. Title of article, in quotation marks
3. Name of periodical, underlined
4. Publication information. This information might include some or all of the following data, which would be presented in the order given below:
   — Series number or name
   — Volume and issue number, in arabic
   — Date of publication
5. Page(s)

How this information is arranged and punctuated, and what information is actually included, depend to a large extent on the nature of the periodical being cited. Consult the examples which follow to determine the appropriate format for a particular source.

## Entries for Articles in Periodicals: Examples

Listed below are guidelines for citing articles in periodicals. Where no specific guideline is given (e.g., for citing works by multiple authors), the entry follows the same general pattern as an entry for a book.

a) **Journal articles:**

**An article published in a journal with continuous pagination throughout the annual volume:** The volume number (in this case, 83) but not the issue number is given.

Bynum, David E. "Themes of the Young Hero in Serbocroatian Oral Epic Tradition." PMLA 83 (1968): 1296-303.

**An article published in a journal that paginates each issue separately:** In this case, the volume number and the issue number are both given. As the example below makes clear, giving both pieces of information is necessary—each of the four issues of volume 19 could have pages numbered from 42 to 60.

Dosman, Edgar J. "Hemispheric Relations in the 1980s: A Perspective from Canada." Journal of Canadian Studies 19.4 (1984): 42-60.

b) **Magazine articles:** In an entry for an article from a weekly or biweekly magazine, the complete date is given in place of volume and issue numbers. If the magazine is published monthly, the month and year published will be considered the complete date. All months except May, June, and July are abbreviated.

Wheeler, Harvey. "The Politics of Ecology." Saturday Review 7 Mar. 1970: 52.

c) **Newspaper articles:** The name of the newspaper should be given as it appears on the masthead, but any article preceding the name (the, a, an) should be dropped. When the place of publication is not part of the newspaper's title, it is added in square brackets after the title. When the newspaper has different editions, the name of the edition that appears on the masthead is placed after the date and preceded by a comma. When each section is paginated separately, the appropriate section letter and page number are given.

If there is no named author for the piece, begin with the title of the article, as in the second example.

```
Milner, Brian. "GATT Decries Growing Wave of
    Protectionism." Globe and Mail [Toronto] 28 Mar.
    1985, Metro ed.: B3.

"Ottawa Cuts Crimp Science, Tech Data." Globe and Mail
    [Toronto] 14 May 1992, Metro ed.: B4.
```

d) **Letter to the Editor or Editorial:** If the letter or editorial is untitled, the appropriate label, neither underlined nor in quotation marks, is given after the name of the author. If the piece is titled, the label is placed after the title.

```
Baichwal, Ravi. Letter. Saturday Night July-Aug. 1990:
    8.

Lapham, Lewis. "Achievement Test." Editorial. Harper's
    July 1991: 10-13.
```

e) **Review (of a book, movie, or live performance):** For a book review, the name of the reviewer is placed first, then the title of the review, then Rev. of followed by the name of the book reviewed, the name of the author of the book, and the periodical information. If the review has no title, Rev. of is placed immediately after the name of the reviewer.

```
Fowles, John. "Literature's Good Soldier." Rev. of
    Ford Madox Ford, by Alan Judd. Atlantic May 1991:
    112-14.
```

For a performance review, relevant information about the production, such as the place of performance and the name of the performing company, is added.

Oliver, Edith. "Antic Dane." Rev. of Hamlet, by
    William Shakespeare. Roundabout Theatre Company,
    Criterion Centre, New York. New Yorker 13 Apr.
    1992: 82.

### Entries for Other Sources: Guidelines and Examples
Entries for other sources such as films, lectures, interviews, and computer software follow the same general pattern as entries for books and published articles.

### Print Material

a) **Government documents:** Often government documents have no stated author, so in a document for which no author is given, the government body is treated as the author. The name of the government author is followed by the title of the document, underlined. When title pages are given in more than one language, only one version need be used. After the title, the available relevant publication information is given (publisher, place and date of publication, pages, etc.). Citing government documents can be complicated, but the Government Documents librarian or another member of the library staff will be able to help you.

Ontario Legislative Assembly. Standing Committee on
    Social Development. Report on Food Banks. 2nd
    session, 34th Parliament. Toronto: Government of
    Ontario, 1990.

Ontario Legislative Assembly. Standing Committee on
    Social Development. Debates. 3rd session, 32nd
    Parliament. Toronto: Government of Ontario, 1983.

## b) Dissertations or theses

**Unpublished:** The title is placed in quotation marks, not underlined. It is followed by a designation such as "Diss." or "M.A. Thesis," the name of the university where it was submitted, and the year of its completion.

Niero, Christine. "Making Stories: Studies in
     Contemporary Canadian Metafiction." Diss.
     Queen's U, 1987.

**Published:** The title is underlined, and the pertinent publication information is given, including a relevant order number.

Finley, A.G. Shipbuilding in St. Martins 1840-1880: A
     Case Study of Family Enterprise on the Fundy Shore.
     M.A. Thesis.  U of New Brunswick, 1980. Ottawa:
     Canadian Theses on Microfiche, 1984.  47732.

## c) Pamphlets:
In general, treat a pamphlet as you would a book. If there is no author, cite the name of the pamphlet first. Often, publication details will be sketchy: use N.p., n.p., and n.d. to indicate missing data.

Human Rights: What to Do about Discrimination or
     Harassment. Peterborough, ON: Trent U, n.d.

## d) Archival material:
The format for citing archival material varies; however, certain pieces of standard information are necessary in all archival citations. The citation must first allow the reader to locate the archival material by identifying the repository and the location of the material within the repository; it must also describe the material as any citation would, giving title, author, date, etc.  For more information, consult Terry Cook, ed. Archival Citations: Suggestions for the Citation of Documents at the Public Archives of Canada (Ottawa: Public Archives, 1983).

In the sample entry below, NA stands for National Archives of Canada, the repository; RG stands for Record Group, the collection within the NA where the material is housed. The material is found on pages 131 and 132 of volume 1846.

```
NA RG10, Vol. 1846, 131, 132, "Treaty No. 3 between
Her Majesty the Queen and the Saulteaux Tribe of
the Ojibbeway Indians at the Northwest Angle of the
Lake of the Woods with Adhesions, 3 October 1873."
```

e) **Legal documents/court cases:** A good standard source for the conventions governing citation of legal documents is the <u>Canadian Guide to Uniform Legal Citation</u> (Toronto: Carswell, 1992), which provides information on documenting statutes, bills, by-laws, regulations, codes, cases, treaties, and international agreements. In general, a citation of a legal document must include the following: identification of case or document, date of document, and information making clear where the document can be found (name, volume, and page of court report, for example).

f) **Material from an information service:** Cite the material from the service much the same way you would cite printed material, giving publication information if the material was previously published. Add the name of the service and the file number at the end of the entry. If the material has not been published previously, cite the service as the publisher. No place of publication is needed. Retain the file number at the end of the citation.

```
Limbrick, Liddy, et al. Peer-Power: Using Peer
Tutoring to Help Low-Progress Readers in Primary
and Secondary Schools. Wellington: New Zealand
Council for Educational Research, 1985. ERIC
ED326858.
```

```
Thomas, Susan B. "Concerns about Gifted Children: A
Paper and Abstract Bibliography." ERIC, 1974. ERIC
ED091083 PS007334.
```

## Non-Print Material

a) **Lectures, addresses, debates:** Following the speaker's name and the title of the lecture, give the name of the course, meeting, or sponsor, the location, and the date. If the title of the presentation is not known, use an accurate descriptive word (e.g., Lecture, Address, Debate). Neither underline this word nor place it in quotation marks.

```
Syrett, John. "Nixon the Great Before Watergate."
Hist. 312, Trent U. 7 Mar. 1984.
```

b) **Personal communications (interviews, letters):** Give the name of the person approached, the appropriate descriptive label (e.g., Personal Interview, Telephone Interview, Personal Letter), and the date of the communication.

```
O'Donoghue, Judith A.   Personal Interview.   9 Apr.
1985.
```

c) **Works of art:**

When the work of art has been reproduced in a book, provide the location and institution where the original can be found, and the publication information for the text in which it is reproduced:

```
Michelangelo. The Rondanini Pieta. Museo del Castello
Sforzesco, Milan. Testament: The Bible as History.
By John Romer. New York: Holt, 1988. Plate 38.
```

When the work of art is viewed in its original form or found in an unpublished source, give the artist's name, the name of the work underlined, the name of the institution housing the artwork, and the location. The location may be cited by city or by city and country when the city is not widely known.

```
Bonheur, Rosa. Plowing Scene. Museum of Fine Arts,
Boston.
```

d) **Films, television and radio programs, slide programs and video-tapes, and sound recordings:** Unlike books and articles, where the author is almost always the creator of what is being cited, in documents such as films, TV programs, and records, many different people contribute to the end product. Whom or what you cite will depend on the nature of your reference. In general, the name of the person or product most directly related to your textual reference is given first (e.g., the name of a film or song, the director or producer of a performance). In addition, your reader will need to know the name of the document (if not already given), production information, and the year of production. The examples below provide some general guidelines.

#### Film—reference to film content
PowWow at Duck Lake.  Prod. John Kemeny and Barrie
  Howells.  Dir. Bonnie Klein.  NFB, 1968.

#### Film—reference to director
Watkins, Peter, writer and dir.  The War Game.  BBC,
  1966.

#### Television program—reference to program
"Land of the Eagle."  Nature.  PBS.  WNED, Buffalo,
  NY.  3 May 1992.

#### Television program—reference to actor
Danza, Tony, actor.  Growing Pains.  ABC.  CHEX,
  Peterborough, ON.  25 Apr. 1992.

#### Sound recording—reference to lyrics (note that David Byrne wrote the lyrics.)
Byrne, David.  "The Big Country."  The Talking Heads:
  More Songs about Buildings and Food.  Sire, 9147-
  6058, 1978.

#### Sound recording—reference to producer (note that the recording artist is given after the title of the album)
Spector, Philip, prod.  Let It Be.  The Beatles.  Apple,
  SW-6386, 1970.

**Video-tape—reference to video-tape content**

<u>Science Study Skills, Section Two: Science Labs</u>.
   Video-tape. Prod. Ann Wetmore and Christine
   Shelton. Mount Saint Vincent University Student
   Affairs Dept., 1991.

e) **Live performance:** Guidelines for performances are much like those for films. Rather than ending with the film company and year of release, performance entries close with the theatre, city, and date of performance.

<u>Counsellors-at-Law</u>. By Elmer Rice. Dir. Neil Munro.
   With Jim Mezon. Shaw Festival, Niagara-on-the-Lake,
   29 May 1992.

f) **Computer software:** Since the authors of most software are not named, usually the title of the software, underlined, is cited first. If the author's name is known, however, it should be placed, surname first, before the title of the program. Follow the title with the version, preceded by the abbreviation "vers.," and the label "Computer software." Complete the reference with the name of the supplier, followed by a comma and the year of issue or copyright.

<u>Wordstar</u>. Computer software. Micropro International,
   1983.

Bricklin, Dan, and Bob Frankston. <u>VisiCalc</u>. Computer
   software. Software Arts, Apr. 1979.

If the program has been designed under contract to a major hard-ware/software manufacturer (e.g., IBM or Apple), add this information after the date, and give the edition number, if known. Also add, if known, the number of kilobytes (e.g., 64KB), the operating system for which the program is designed (e.g., IBM PC-DOS 2.10), and the form of the program (cartridge, cassette, or, more commonly, disk). Separate each of these items with a comma and put a period at the end:

Microsoft Disk Operating System.   Computer software.
   Microsoft Corp., Sept. 1983.   IBM, IBM PC-DOS 2.10,
   disk.

Note that in some cases you will find that when a major hard-ware/software manufacturer owns the program, the manufacturer's name is listed first:

Tandy. Studymate: The Grade Booster. Ver. 2.1.
   Computer Software. Compu-Teach Corp, 1990. IBM PC.
   Disk.

# PARENTHETICAL DOCUMENTATION: STYLE B (APA STYLE)

Style B, which is used predominantly in the social and natural sciences, allows for greater emphasis on the year in which material has been published. It is different from Style A in three main ways:

—The date of publication appears in a parenthetical citation, along with the names of the authors and the portion of the work (page, figure, or chapter number) being cited if required.

—The list of works cited at the end of a paper is headed "References" or "References Cited."

—The date of publication appears immediately after the name(s) of the author(s) in this list of references.

Within Style B, the punctuation, capitalization, and form of citations in the text and in the list of references vary between and within disciplines. Because there is a uniform method of documentation in psychology, described in the third edition of the <u>Publication Manual of the American Psychological Association</u>, this method will form the basis for our presentation of Style B. To cite in other social or natural science courses, students should consult the "List of Documentation Methods by Academic Discipline" to discover whether there are any variations from Style B in a discipline.

## REFERENCES IN THE TEXT

### Guidelines
The date information appears is more relevant for the sciences than for the humanities. Thus, in Style B, the publication date of cited material must be given, along with the names of the authors of this material. This information may be given either in a parenthetical citation or in the text of the essay itself:

A later study showed that this feature was absent in the second group (Woodsworth, 1977).

Woodsworth (1977) found that this feature was absent in the second group.

In 1977, Woodsworth found that this feature was absent in the second group.

Although it is usual to give only the author and date of publication when referring to a source, it is sometimes necessary to indicate that the reference is to a specific part of a source, to pages (pp.), a page (p.), a chapter (chap.), or a figure (Fig.). In such cases, the parenthetical citation, or the text of the essay, must include reference to the portion of the source. Even though referring to a part of a source is quite rare in psychology papers, page references must be given for direct quotations:

A subsequent experiment showed "no connection between type of settlement and satisfaction" (Vidmar, 1985, p. 139).

Vidmar (1985) found "no connection between type of settlement and satisfaction" (p. 139).

In 1985, Vidmar found "no connection between type of settlement and satisfaction" (p. 139).

Note that these examples of parenthetical citation avoid repeating information that is already provided in the text of the essay, outside the parenthetical citation.

### Examples of Standard Form

a) **References to one work by a single author:**

People are usually not aware of their own cultural characteristics and conditioning because it is difficult to see that which is closest (Hall, 1976).

According to anthropologist Edward Hall (1976), people are usually not aware of their own cultural characteristics and conditioning because it is difficult to see that which is closest.

b) **References to one work by two or more authors:**

*Two authors:* Cite both names always, and use an ampersand (&) rather than the word "and" to join those names.

An earlier study (Snyder & Monson, 1975) reported that high self-monitors estimated that they would show more variability across situations in generosity and honesty.

Snyder and Monson (1975) also determined that high self-monitors estimated that they would show more variability across situations in hostility.

*More than two authors and fewer than six:* Cite all names in the first reference and use the surname of the first author followed by "et al." in subsequent references.

*First reference:*

One paper (Gergen, Gergen, & Morse, 1972) hypothesizes that religious beliefs affect the use of illegal drugs and alcohol.

Gergen, Gergen, and Morse (1972) studied the correlation between religious beliefs and the use of illegal drugs and alcohol.

*Subsequent references:*

The relevance of religious beliefs to premarital sex has also been investigated (Gergen et al., 1972).

Gergen et al. (1972) also studied the relevance of religious beliefs to premarital sex.

*Six authors or more:* Cite the surname of the first author followed by "et al." unless you are citing two references with six or more authors that would be shortened to the same form. In this case, cite as many authors as necessary to distinguish between the two references.

One group attempted to modify the behaviour of hyperactive children through drug therapy (Gittelman-Klein et al., 1980).

Gittelman-Klein et al. (1980) attempted to modify the behaviour of hyperactive children through drug therapy.

c) **References to corporate authors:**

*First citation:*

In the early seventies, the future of Canadian psychology looked bright (Canadian Psychological Association [CPA], 1971).

According to the Canadian Psychological Association (CPA) (1971), the future of Canadian psychology looked bright in the early seventies.

*Subsequent references:*

This study (CPA, 1971) also investigated employment opportunities for psychologists.

The study by the CPA (1971) also investigated employment opportunities for psychologists.

d) **References to a source with no author or with an anonymous author:**

*No author:* Cite the first two or three words of the title in place of the author's name. Use double quotation marks when citing the title of an article or chapter and underline the title of a book, pamphlet, or periodical.

Many delegates spoke about the anti-feminist reactions of the media ("Feminist feedback," 1992).

<u>Resources for persons with special needs</u> (1991) describes services provided to students with physical, sensory, or learning disabilities.

*An author designated as anonymous:* Cite the word "Anonymous" in place of the author's name.

The experiment found no correlation between gender and computer phobia (Anonymous, 1983).

e) **References to different works with the same author and date:** Use the suffixes a, b, c, etc. to distinguish between works by the same author(s) with the same publication date.

The antisocial behaviour of hyperactive children has also been studied (Cantwell, 1978a).

Cantwell (1978b) determined the usefulness of CNS activating drugs in the treatment of hyperactivity.

f) **References to two or more works within a single set of parentheses:** Such references are necessary to cite ideas expressed in several sources, more than one publication of an author, or the results of a number of experiments documented in various articles:

Eye-voice studies (Levin & Kaplan, 1968; Tinker, 1958) show that the eye can read ahead of the voice.

*Same author(s) of several works:* Arrange chronologically.

```
(Wong, 1979, 1986, 1987)
(Decker & DeFries, 1980, 1981)
```

*Same author(s) of several works with the same publication date:* Arrange chronologically using the suffixes a, b, c, etc.

```
(Stanovich, 1980, 1983a, 1983b, 1986)
(Woodcock & Johnson, 1977a, 1977b)
```

*Different authors:* Arrange in alphabetical order and separate by semicolons.

```
(Rawson, 1986; Shepherd, 1980; Torgesen & Dice,
1980)
```

*Different authors of several works:* Arrange in alphabetical order, and, within that alphabetical arrangement, arrange chronologically.

```
(Decker & DeFries, 1980, 1981; Stanovich,
1983a, 1983b)
(Rawson, 1986; Shepherd, 1980; Woodcock &
Johnson, 1977a, 1977b)
```

g) **References to a work you have not read:** Occasionally, you must refer to something that you have not read but that has been cited or quoted in a work that you have read. It is best to do this only when absolutely necessary.

```
(McKinney, 1983, as cited in Johnson, 1988, p. 81)
(Wicker, 1969, as quoted in Zanna, Olson, & Fazio,
1980, p. 107)
```

# REFERENCES (FOR STYLE B)

Each discipline that uses Style B has its own format for entries in the list of references. Therefore, **unless writing a paper for psychology, you should consult the individual subject examples given on pages 119 to 143.** These examples will show you how to make use of and modify the following information for disciplines other than psychology.

**General rules:**

1. All the references cited in the text must appear in the list of references, and each entry in this list must be cited in the text. Make sure that the reference in the text to a work corresponds to the reference to that work in the reference list.

2. The list of references cited is headed "References," and entries in the list are always arranged alphabetically by author's last name. Last names are always listed before first names, which are represented by initials.

3. If there is more than one author, list all the authors' names in the reference list, last name first.

4. If two or more works by the same author(s) have been used, list them chronologically by year of publication, rather than alphabetically by title; if they were published in the same year, arrange them alphabetically by title and distinguish each by the addition of a letter to the date (e.g., 1978a, 1978b).

5. When arranging several works by the same first author, single-author entries precede multiple-author entries. Multiple-author entries with the same first author and different subsequent authors are arranged alphabetically.

**Entries for Books and Sections of Books: Guidelines and Examples**

Pay careful attention to the order of information within entries and to punctuation, spacing, and capitalization.

*Books or Pamphlets*
a) **By single authors:** The author's last name is listed first and is followed by the author's initials. The date of publication appears in

parentheses, the book's title is underlined, and the place of publication is separated from the name of the publisher by a colon. Note that, other than proper nouns, only the first word of the title or the first word after a colon in the title is capitalized.

Hall, E. T. (1976). <u>Beyond culture</u>. Garden City, NY: Anchor Press.

b) **By two or more authors:**

Luthans, F., & Kreitner, R. (1985). <u>Organizational behavior: Modification and beyond</u>. Glenview, IL: Scott, Foresman.

c) **Corporate authors:**

Canadian Psychological Association. (1971). <u>The future of Canadian psychology</u>. Ottawa: Science Council of Canada.

d) **With an editor or editors:** The abbreviation "Ed." or "Eds." is used to refer to the editor or editors.

Fishbein, M. (Ed.). (1967). <u>Readings in attitude theory and measurement</u>. New York: Wiley.

Berry, J. W., & Wilde, G. J. S. (Eds.). (1972). <u>Social psychology: The Canadian context</u>. Toronto: McClelland & Stewart.

e) **With no author or editor:**

<u>Resources for persons with special needs</u>. (1991). Peterborough, ON: Trent University Communications Department.

## f) Specific editions or volumes:

Cohen, J. (1977). <u>Statistical power analysis for the behavioral sciences</u> (rev. ed.). New York: Academic Press.

Wren, D. (1979). <u>The evolution of management thought</u> (2nd ed.). New York: Wiley.

Cummings, L., & Straw, B. M. (Eds.). (1981). <u>Research in organizational behavior</u> (Vol. 3). Greenwich, CT: JAI Press.

## *Sections of Books*

a) **Articles or chapters in an edited book:** Note that last names and initials are given for all authors and editors and that the editors' names are given with initials first, and last names last. The abbreviation "Ed." or "Eds." is used to refer to the editor or editors.

Gittelman-Klein, R., Abikoff, H., Pollack, E., Klein, D. F., Katz, S., & Mattes, J. (1980). A controlled trial of   behavior modification and methyl-phenidate in hyperactive children. In C. K. Whalen & C. K. Henker (Eds.), <u>Hyperactive children: The social ecology of identification and treatment</u> (pp. 211-243). New York: Academic Press.

Regan, D. T. (1978). Attributional aspects of interpersonal attraction. In J. H. Harvey, W. J. Ickes, & R. F. Kidd (Eds.), <u>New directions in attribution research</u> (Vol. 2, pp. 207-233). Hillsdale, NJ: Lawrence Erlbaum.

b) **Contributions to published proceedings of meetings or symposia:**
Contributions to regularly published proceedings are treated as articles
in periodicals (see (a) below and page 107(b) and (c)). Note that the
symposium or conference name is capitalized because it is a proper
noun.

Cotman, C. W., & Lynch, G. F. (1988). The neurobiology
    of learning and memory. In J. F. Kavanagh & T. J.
    Truss (Eds.), <u>Proceedings of the National
    Conference on Learning Disabilities</u> (pp. 1-69).
    Parkton, MD: York Press.

### Entries for Articles in Periodicals: Guidelines and Examples

Note that the full titles of periodicals are given and that, unlike the titles of
books or articles, these titles are written with all major words capitalized.
All the authors of an article are listed as well. Pay close attention to the
details of punctuation, capitalization, and spacing exemplified. Remember
that the abbreviation "p." or "pp." for page or pages is not used in entries
for journals. On the other hand, this abbreviation is used in entries for
magazine and newspaper articles.

### Journals, Magazines, and Newspapers

a) **Articles in journals paginated by volume:** There are no double
quotation marks around the title of the article, the title and the volume
number of the journal are underlined, and there is no abbreviation "p."
or "pp."

Gergen, M. K., Gergen, K. J., & Morse, S. J. (1972).
    Correlates of marijuana use among college students.
    <u>Journal of Applied Social Psychology</u>, <u>2</u>, 1-16.

Snyder, M., & Monson, T. C. (1975). Persons,
    situations, and the control of social behavior.
    <u>Journal of Personality and Social Psychology</u>,
    <u>32</u>, 637-644.

b) **Articles in journals paginated by issue:** The issue number is listed in parentheses after the volume number.

Vidmar, N. (1985). An assessment of mediation in a small claims court. <u>Journal of Social Issues</u>, <u>41</u>(2), 127-144.

Glenn, E. S., Witmeyer, D., & Stevenson, K. A. (1977). Cultural styles of persuasion. <u>International Journal of Intercultural Relations</u>, <u>1</u>(3), 52-66.

c) **Contributions to annually published proceedings:** These are treated as if they were articles in an annually published periodical.

Zabrack, M., & Miller, N. (1972). Group aggression: The effects of friendship ties and anonymity. <u>Proceedings of the 80th Annual Convention of the American Psychological Association</u>, <u>7</u>, 211-212.

d) **Magazine articles:** The month or season of the issue is given with the date of publication, and sometimes the day of publication is also necessary. The abbreviation "p." or "pp." is used.

Fischman, J. (1987, February). Type A on trial. <u>Psychology Today</u>, pp. 42-50.

e) **Newspaper articles:** The full date of publication appears in parentheses and the abbreviation "p." or "pp." is used. Note also that discontinuous pages would be indicated as follows: pp. 1, 16, 20.

*With an author:*

Taylor, K. (1991, November 8). Love among the desks — it doesn't have to be harassment. <u>The Globe and Mail</u>, p. A15.

*Without an author:*

Feminist feedback. (1992, May 14). <u>The Globe and Mail</u>,
 p. C4.

f) **Letters to the editor or editorials:** If the letter or editorial is titled,
 place the title directly after the publication date and follow it with a
 description in square brackets. If untitled, simply follow the date with
 the description in square brackets. Other conventions are dictated by
 the type of periodical in which the letter or editorial is published.

*Titled:*

Seabrooke, E. (1991, August 22). Stop the swarming
 [Letter to the editor]. <u>Peterborough Examiner</u>,
 p. 4.

Doyle, K. (1990, October 8). The road to anarchy
 [Editorial]. <u>Maclean's</u>, p. 4.

*Untitled:*

Heale, M. (1991). [Letter to the editor]. <u>Journal of
 the History of the Behavioral Sciences</u>, <u>27</u>(1),
 76-77.

Newson, J. (1991, July 1). [Letter to the editor].
 <u>Maclean's</u>, p. 7.

Winocur, G. (1989). [Editorial]. <u>Canadian Journal of
 Psychology</u>, <u>43</u>, i-ii.

g) **Reviews:** If the review of the book or film is titled, list the title after
 the publication date and follow it with a description in square brackets.
 For an untitled review, place the description in brackets after the
 publication date; retain the brackets to indicate that what is enclosed is
 a description of form and content, not a title. Other conventions are
 dictated by the type of periodical in which the review is published.

*Titled:*

Hoffman, P. (1988, December). Fun with Kurt and Bert
    [Review of Labyrinths of reason]. <u>Atlantic</u>, pp.
    88-91.

*Untitled:*

Irujo, S. (1991). [Review of <u>Forked tongue: The
    politics of bilingual education</u>]. <u>TESOL Quarterly</u>,
    <u>25</u>(1), 150-156.

h) **Published interviews:** Entries for titled and untitled interviews follow
   the same conventions as entries for titled and untitled reviews. If the
   interview is titled, then the title follows the publication date and is
   followed by a description in square brackets. If the interview is
   untitled, the description, in square brackets, follows the publication
   date. Other conventions are dictated by the type of periodical in which
   the interview is published.

*Titled:*

Lipstein, O. (1992, May/June). Yesterday, today, and
    tomorrow    [Interview with Nicholas Charney,
    founder of <u>Psychology Today</u>]. <u>Psychology Today</u>,
    pp. 20, 31.

*Untitled:*

Dettmer, P. (1991). [Interview with Peter D.
    Rosenstein]. <u>Gifted Child Quarterly</u>, <u>35</u>, 179-181.

g) **An abstract only:** When only an abstract is used as a source, cite the
   collection of abstracts in parentheses at the end of the entry. If the
   publication date of the original publication is different from the
   publication date of the abstract, cite both dates separated by a slash and
   place the original publication date first.

Day, M. C. (1980/1981). Selective attention by
    children and adults to pictures specified by color.
    <u>Journal of Experimental Child Psychology</u>, <u>30</u>,
    277-289. (From <u>Psychological Abstracts</u>, 1981, <u>65</u>,
    Abstract No. 1024)

## Entries for Other Sources: Guidelines and Examples

Entries for other sorts of material, both print and non-print, follow the same general pattern as those for books, sections of books, and articles in periodicals.

### Print Material

a) **Government documents:**

*With a person as author:*

Allen, G.P. (1979) <u>Days to remember: Observances of significance in our multicultural society</u>. Toronto: Ontario Ministry of Culture and Recreation.

*With a government body as author:*

Ontario. Ministry of Education. (1980). <u>Race, religion, and culture in Ontario school materials: Suggestions for authors and publishers</u>. Toronto: Queen's Printer for Ontario.

b) **Doctoral dissertations and master's theses:**

*Doctoral dissertations not abstracted in <u>Dissertation Abstracts International</u>:*

Gardner, R. C. (1960). <u>Motivational variables in second-language acquisition</u>. Unpublished doctoral dissertation, McGill University, Montreal.

*Master's theses not abstracted in <u>Masters Abstracts</u>:*

Sheppard, A. (1980) <u>Monologue and dialogue speech of language-impaired children in clinic and home settings: Semantic, conversational and syntactic characteristics</u>. Unpublished master's thesis, University of Western Ontario, London, ON.

*Doctoral dissertations obtained from the university and abstracted in Dissertation Abstracts International:*

Hudson, S. A. (1986). Context and children's writing (Doctoral dissertation, University of Georgia, 1985). Dissertation Abstracts International, 45, 1669A.

*Doctoral dissertations or master's theses abstracted in either Dissertation Abstracts International or Masters Abstracts and obtained on university microfilm:*

Klein, R. E. (1979). Household type and extended kinship in Taiwan. Dissertation Abstracts International, 39, 6354A- 6355A. (University Microfilms No. 79-07,108)

## Non-Print Material

The APA gives only a few examples and guidelines regarding the documentation of non-print material, but the following information is consistent with that given.

a) **Films, sound recordings, video-tapes, slides, and art works:** The names and the functions of the originators or primary contributors are listed first. These are followed by the year of production, the title of the work, and the medium, which is listed in square brackets immediately after the title. It is also important to give the location and name of the distributor.

*Films:*

Kemeny, J. (Producer), Howells, B. (Producer), & Klein, B. (Director). (1968). PowWow at Duck Lake [Film]. Ottawa: National Film Board of Canada.

Watkins, P. (Writer and Director). (1966). The war game [Film]. London: British Broadcasting Corporation.

*Sound recordings:* Give a number for a recording after the medium if this number is needed for identification and retrieval. Use parentheses around the medium and the number when a number is necessary. If you do not give a number, use square brackets around the medium.

Jones, J. F. (Speaker). (1992). <u>Theories of language acquisition</u> (Cassette Recording No. 5941). Toronto: Association for Bilingualism.

Byrne, D. (Lyricist). (1978). <u>The Talking Heads: More songs about buildings and food</u> [Sound Recording]. New York: Sire.

*Videotapes:*

Wetmore, A. (Producer), & Shelton, C. (Producer). (1991). <u>Science study skills, section two: Science labs</u> [Videotape]. Halifax, NS: Mount Saint Vincent University Student Affairs Department.

*Works of art:*

Bonheur, R. (Artist). (1853). <u>Horse market</u> [Painting]. New York: Metropolitan Museum.

b) **Computer programs:** Give the primary contributor as the author. After the date and title, indicate within square brackets that the source is a computer program. After the location and name of the organization that produced the program, list in parentheses any information necessary to retrieve or identify the program.

Marcus, S. (1989). <u>Hypershelf: Version 2.0</u> [Computer program]. Santa Barbara, CA: South Coast Writing Project.

Smyth, R. M. (1982). <u>Mendelian genetics</u> [Computer program]. Georgetown, ON: Merlan Scientific Ltd. (Merlan Biology Series No. 2; Merlan Scientific Ltd. Catalogue No. 23A200)

c) **Machine-readable data files:**

Statistics Canada (1992). <u>Canadian socio-economic information management system (CANSIM): Consumer price indexes for Canada, monthly record: Food</u> [Machine-readable data file on June 1992 CD-ROM disk: Matrix 001922, Data No. 484000]. Ottawa: Statistics Canada.

# NUMBER-REFERENCE METHOD OF DOCUMENTATION (CBE STYLE)

In the number-reference method of documentation, numbers inserted in the text correspond to the numbered sources listed in the list of references, which appears at the end of the paper. This method of documentation is used in the medical sciences, chemistry, computer science, mathematics, and physics, although use of parenthetical documentation (usually a form of Style B) is also acceptable in most of these disciplines. It is important to understand that there is no single model of the number-reference method of documentation. To give you a general understanding of this method, however, we have used the form recommended by the Council of Biology Editors in the CBE Style Manual, 4th edition.

## CBE Format

According to CBE format, entries in the list of references are arranged in one of two ways: 1) in sequence according to the first reference to each source in the text or 2) alphabetically by author. All entries are assigned a number, and these numbers, rather than the names of authors, are placed in parentheses within the text when citing a source. Sample One shows in-text citations and a list of references in which entries are arranged in order of their first mention in the text. Sample Two shows in-text citations and a list of references in which entries are arranged alphabetically by author and numbered sequentially. Note that when quoting a source, you add page numbers to your in-text citation.

1. Sample One

**Citations in the body of the paper:**

> Contrary to popular belief, cancer cells do not grow faster than normal cells (1). This erroneous conception may have its origins in the fact that when a cancer cell divides, both daughter cells retain their capacity to divide and are free from normal control mechanisms (2). The stage at which this growth occurs is often called the tumour initiation phase (1,3). This stage may be followed

by the tumour promotion phase and the selection
phase. However, the first step toward tumour
growth, initiation, does not necessarily lead to
cancer; if the second step (promotion) fails to
take place, the latent tumour cell will not be
attained (2). In fact, "interruption of the
metastatic cascade at any of these steps can
prevent the production of clinically symptomatic
metastasis" (4, p.99).

### Entries in the list of references:

1.  Doll, R.; Peto, R. The causes of cancer:
    quantitative estimates of avoidable risks of
    cancer in the United States today. New York:
    Oxford University Press; 1981.

2.  Rather, L. J. The genesis of cancer: a study in
    the history of ideas. Baltimore: Johns Hopkins
    University Press; 1978.

3.  Friedewald, W. F.; Rous, P. The initiating and
    promoting elements in tumour production. J.
    Exper. Med. 80: 101-125; 1944.

4.  Liotta, L. A.; Stetler-Stevenson, W. G.
    Principles of molecular cell biology of cancer:
    cancer metastasis. DeVita, V. T.; Hellman, S.;
    Rosenberg, S. A. eds. Cancer: principles and
    practice of oncology. 3rd ed. Vol 1.
    Philadelphia: J. B. Lippincott Company;
    1989: 98-115.

## 2. Sample Two

### Citations in the body of the paper:

Contrary to popular belief, cancer cells do not grow faster than normal cells (1). This erroneous conception may have its origins in the fact that when a cancer cell divides, both daughter cells retain their capacity to divide and are free from normal control mechanisms (4). The stage at which this growth occurs is often called the tumour initiation phase (1,2). This stage may be followed by the tumour promotion phase and the selection phase. However, the first step toward tumour growth, initiation, does not necessarily lead to cancer; if the second step (promotion) fails to take place, the latent tumour cell will not be attained (4). In fact, "interruption of the metastatic cascade at any of these steps can prevent the production of clinically symptomatic metastasis" (3, p.99).

### Entries in the list of references:

1. Doll, R.; Peto, R. The causes of cancer: quantitative estimates of avoidable risks of cancer in the United States today. New York: Oxford University Press; 1981.

2. Friedewald, W. F.; Rous, P. The initiating and promoting elements in tumour production. J. Exper. Med. 80:101-125; 1944.

3. Liotta, L. A.; Stetler-Stevenson, W. G. Principles of molecular cell biology of cancer: cancer metastasis. DeVita, V. T.; Hellman, S.; Rosenberg, S. A. eds. Cancer: principles and practice of oncology. 3rd ed. Vol 1. Philadelphia: J. B. Lippincott Company; 1989: 98-115.

4. Rather, L. J. The genesis of cancer: a study in the history of ideas. Baltimore: Johns Hopkins University Press; 1978.

## Variations

There is a great variation in the format of the number-reference method of documentation, and for this reason, most professional societies and many scholarly journals in the sciences produce style sheets explaining the format acceptable for members or contributors. You will find that the form of in-text citations (both first and subsequent references) and the form and order of entries in the list of references can vary considerably.

### 1. In-Text Citations: Variations

In-text citations usually give the number of the entry in parentheses, in square brackets, or as a superscript (small print above the regular line of print).

### a)  Using parentheses:

Many scientists have performed similar experiments (2,3,4).

or

Many scientists have performed similar experiments (2-4).

### b)  Using square brackets:

Many scientists have performed similar experiments [2,3,4].

or

Many scientists have performed similar experiments [2-4].

### c) Using superscript numbers:

Many scientists have performed similar
experiments.[2,3,4]

**or**

Many scientists have performed similar
experiments.[2-4]

### 2. Subsequent References: Variations

Subsequent references to the same source usually use the same number as
the first reference:

### a) Using parentheses:

One researcher (3) made the most conclusive
investigation.

### b) Using square brackets:

One researcher [3] made the most conclusive
investigation.

### c) Using superscript numbers:

One researcher[3] made the most conclusive
investigation.

Subsequent references are sometimes treated differently when using a
form of the number-reference system that does not allow for page numbers
or portions of sources to be included in the in-text citations. As
demonstrated earlier, the CBE format enables the writer to include
information about what part of a source is being cited or quoted within the
in-text citation:

In fact, "interruption of the metastatic cascade at
any of these steps can prevent the production of
clinically symptomatic metastasis" (3, p.99).

When this information can be included, even subsequent references that refer to different portions of a source can use the same number as the first reference to that source. However, when this information cannot be included in the in-text citation and a different page number must be given in a reference to a source already cited, the subsequent reference is treated as a first reference and the author, title, and publication information, as well as the relevant page number(s), are given in the new entry.

3. The List of References: Variations

The format and ordering of the list of references also varies between disciplines and among scholarly journals within the same discipline. This list is always placed at the end of the paper or article and is titled "References," "Literature Cited," "References Cited," or a similar term. The <u>CBE Style Manual</u> indicates that authors' last names should be listed first in this list and that, sometimes, entries should be arranged alphabetically. However, in most other variations of the number-reference method, neither alphabetizing entries within the list of references nor putting the last names of authors before their first in this list is necessary. This is because a number is sufficient to make a connection between a reference in the text of a paper and an entry in the list of references. **Be sure that you consult the section "List of Documentation Methods by Academic Discipline" for information on the various forms of the number-reference system acceptable in chemistry, computer science, mathematics, and physics.**

# PART V:
# LIST OF DOCUMENTATION
# METHODS BY ACADEMIC
## ——————— DISCIPLINE ———————

The list below indicates which documentation method each discipline prefers. Specific examples are given only where the style of documentation used by a discipline differs in some respect from the styles outlined in "Part IV: Documentation." The examples given always include a published book, an article in a book, and an article in a journal; sometimes, other examples are given, but you are expected to adapt other types of entries to the format illustrated. If you require further information, consult your instructor or a leading journal in the field. Some journals that you might want to consult are also listed.

## Administrative Studies
Any one of the four styles of documentation described in this text, as long as it is used correctly and consistently, is acceptable in administrative studies. We suggest that you follow the variation of Style B described in the section "Economics," which is on page 130-132.

## Anthropology/Archaeology
Anthropology and archaeology students should modify Style B in the following ways.

### *References in the Text*
1. Commas are eliminated between the elements of the parenthetical citation.

2. A colon is used in place of "p." when a page reference is given.

3. The ampersand (&) is replaced by an "and" in references having two authors.

4. The abbreviation "et al." is used in parenthetical citations only to refer to works having three or more authors.

Remember that all ideas and data taken from others must be acknowledged in either the text of a paper or in a parenthetical citation. However, do not repeat the name(s) of the author(s) or the publication date of an item in a parenthetical citation if either is mentioned in the text of the paper.

### References to certain portions of sources:

The !Kung elders believe themselves entitled to the necessities of life because they are full members of !Kung society:

> !Kung elders do not see themselves as burdens.... They expect others to care for them when they can no longer do so. Entitlement to care is naturalized within the culture. Elders do not have to negotiate care as if it were a favor; rather it is perceived as a right. (Rosenberg 1990:29)

This is what Ingold calls a "different kind of sociality" (1990:130-131).

The earliest recorded reference to the BaMbuti is in a record of an expedition sent from Egypt in the Fourth Dynasty to discover the source of the Nile (Turnbull 1961:15).

### References to whole sources:

I will compare Salisbury's 1966 study of myth creation in New Guinea with Mead's <u>Growing up in New Guinea</u>, published in 1930.

Headland and Reid (1989) investigate the relations between hunter-gatherers and their neighbors, and Hawkes et al. (1982) study the Ache of Eastern Paraguay to discover why hunters gather.

In recent times, indigenous peoples have spoken to the public directly in various settings, including the courts (Sterritt 1989; People of 'Ksan 1980; Gisday Wa and Delgum Uukw 1989).

### List of References
The list of references is usually entitled "References Cited," and includes only those items referred to in the body of the paper. This list follows Style B in all but punctuation and physical layout. Note that in most areas of anthropology titles of books and journals are not underlined in the "References Cited" section. However, when writing an archaeology paper, you should probably underline these titles. Consult your instructor.

## ANTHROPOLOGY
### References Cited

Headland, Tom, and Lawrence Reid
    1989 Hunter Gatherers and Their Neighbors from Prehistory to the Present. Current Anthropology 30:43-66.

Ingold, Tim
    1986a The Appropriation of Nature: Essays on Human Ecology and Social Relations. Manchester: Manchester University Press.

    1986b Evolution and Social Life. Cambridge: Cambridge University Press.

    1990 Comment on "Foragers, Genuine or Spurious: Situating the Kalahari San in History," by J. Solway and R. Lee. Current Anthropology 31: 130-131.

Kent, Susan, ed.
    1989 Farmers as Hunters: Implications of Sedentism. Cambridge: Cambridge University Press.

People of 'Ksan
    1980 Gathering What the Great Nature Provided: Food Traditions of the Gitksan. Vancouver: Douglas and McIntyre.

Rosenberg, Harriet G.
    1990 Complaint Discourse, Aging, and Caregiving among the !Kung San of Botswana. In The Cultural Context of Aging. Jay Sokolovsky, ed. pp. 19-41. New York: Bergin and Garvey.

ARCHAEOLOGY

References Cited

Headland, Tom, and Lawrence Reid
   1989   Hunter Gatherers and Their Neighbors from
   Prehistory to the Present.   Current Anthropology
   30:43-66.

Ingold, Tim
   1986a   The Appropriation of Nature: Essays on Human
   Ecology and Social Relations. Manchester:
   Manchester University Press.
   1986b   Evolution and Social Life. Cambridge:
   Cambridge University Press.
   1990   Comment on "Foragers, Genuine or Spurious:
   Situating the Kalahari San in History," by J.
   Solway and R. Lee. Current Anthropology 31:
   130-131.

Kent, Susan, ed.
   1989   Farmers as Hunters: Implications of
   Sedentism. Cambridge: Cambridge University Press.

People of 'Ksan
   1980   Gathering What the Great Nature Provided:
   Food Traditions of the Gitksan. Vancouver:
   Douglas and McIntyre.

Rosenberg, Harriet G.
   1990   Complaint Discourse, Aging, and Caregiving
   among the !Kung San of Botswana. In The Cultural
   Context of Aging. Jay Sokolovsky, ed. pp. 19-41.
   New York: Bergin and Garvey.

Further details and examples can be found in the guides published either in
American Anthropologist 89:272-275 (for anthropological papers) or in
American Antiquity 48:429-442 (for archaeological papers).

## Biology

Although it is sometimes appropriate to use that form of the number-reference method recommended by the Council of Biology Editors, usually biology uses a form of Style B, but modifies that style in various ways. As long as students follow the documentation method required by a reputable Canadian journal in the field, they should find that their papers are acceptable. One such method, based on that used in the <u>Canadian Journal of Zoology</u>, is outlined below. Another, based on the method recommended by the <u>Canadian Journal of Fisheries and Aquatic Sciences</u>, is shown under the heading "Environmental and Resource Studies."

### *References in the Text*

1. There is no comma between the name of the author and the date of publication: (Banfield 1974).

2. When referring to a certain portion of a source (e.g., page, figure, table), separate this reference from the date of publication with a comma: (Thomas 1990, p. 156).

3. In references to works having two authors, use "and" rather than an ampersand: (Dustin and Saunders 1990).

4. In references to works having more than two authors, use "et al." in the <u>parenthetical citation</u>: (McCormick et al. 1987). Do not use "et al." in the list of references cited. Write out all the authors' names.

In biological journals, using quotations and, consequently, referring to portions of sources is very rare. However, all ideas and information taken from others must be documented. Also remember that if you mention the author and the date of publication of your source in the text of your paper, it is not necessary to repeat this information in a parenthetical citation.

### References to certain portions of texts:

<u>Dreissena</u> populations quickly recover from crashes (Ramcharan et al. 1992, fig. 1).

Thomas cannot believe that there is "something fundamentally unnatural, or intrinsically wrong, or hazardous for the species in the ambition that drives us all to reach a comprehensive understanding of nature, including ourselves" (1990, p. 156).

As early as 1962, Rachel Carson wrote, "Future generations are unlikely to condone our lack of prudent concern for the integrity of the natural world that supports all life" (p. 13).

**References to whole texts:**
Dustin and Saunders' research on the photoperiod and aspects of smolting, published in 1990, acknowledged the work of McCormick et al. that was published in 1987.

Research on snapping turtles (Chelydra serpentina) has benefitted from the contributions of Galbraith and Brooks (1987a, 1987b, 1989).

In the 1980s, much work on the reproductive physiology of fish involved the study of steroids (Fostier et al. 1983; Scott and Canario 1987).

### *List of References*
Only those sources cited in your paper are included in the list of references, which usually has the heading "References." The list itself follows the order of Style B; however, within entries there are variations in order, punctuation, underlining, and format. Three notable differences are that there are no parentheses around the date of publication, that titles are not underlined, and that the publisher is listed before the place of publication. Notice also that journal titles are abbreviated in the form given in CASSI or in Serial Sources for the BIOSIS Data Base and that the names of genera and species are underlined to indicate that they should appear in italics.

# DOCUMENTATION BY DISCIPLINE

## References

Anonymous. 1987. Canadian Forestry Service Management Plan for 1986.

Banfield, A. W. F. 1974. The mammals of Canada. University of Toronto Press, Toronto.

Canadian Hydrographic Service, 1988. Canadian tide and current tables. Vol. 4. Fisheries and Oceans Canada, Ottawa.

Dustin, J., and Saunders, R. L. 1990. The entrainment role of photoperiod on hypoosmoregulatory and growth-related aspects of smolting in Atlantic salmon (Salmo salar). Can. J. Zool. 68: 707-715.

Fay, F. H. 1982. Ecology and biology of the Pacific walrus. North American Fauna No. 74. U.S. Fish and Wildlife Service, Washington, D.C.

Fostier, A. Jalabert, B., Billard, R., Breton, B., and Zohar, Y. 1983. The gonadal steroids. In Fish physiology, Vol 9A. Edited by W. S. Hoar, D. J. Randall, and E. M. Donaldson. Academic Press, New York. pp. 277-372.

Galbraith, D. A., and Brooks, R. J. 1987a. Survivorship of adult females in a northern population of common snapping turtles, Chelydra serpentina. Can. J. Zool. 65: 1581-1586.

Galbraith, D. A., and Brooks, R. J. 1987b. Addition of annual growth lines in adult snapping turtles, Chelydra serpentina. J. Herpetol. 21: 359-363.

Galbraith, D. A., and Brooks, R. J. 1989. Age estimates for snapping turtles. J. Wildl. Manage. 58: 502-508.

Parsons, J. L. 1977. Metabolic studies on ringed seals (Phoca hispida). M.Sc. thesis, Department of Pathology, University of Guelph, Guelph, Ont.

Scott, A. P., and Canario, A. V. M. 1987. Status of oocyte maturation-inducing steroids in teleosts. <u>In</u> Proceedings of the Third International Symposium on Reproductive Physiology of Fish, 2-7 August 1987, St. John's, Nfld. <u>Edited by</u> D. R. Idler, L. W. Crim, and J. M. Walsh. Memorial University, St. John's, Nfld. pp. 224-234.

Whitworth, T. L. 1976. Host and habitat preferences, life history, pathogenicity, and population regulation in species of <u>Protocalliphora</u> Hough (Diptera: Calliphoridae). Ph.D. dissertation, Utah State University, Logan.

Use either the <u>Canadian Journal of Zoology</u> or the <u>Canadian Journal of Botany</u> as a model for other kinds of references.

## Canadian Studies
In interdisciplinary studies such as Canadian studies, use the documentation method indicated in the course syllabus. If none is given, it is best to follow the documentation method preferred in the discipline which most informs the essay you are writing. For example, in an historical essay, use the footnoting/bibliography method; in an economics essay, the form of Style B described under "Economics" would be appropriate; in an essay based on Canadian literature, you would probably want to choose either Style A or the footnoting/bibliography method.

## Chemistry
Chemistry usually uses a form of the number-reference method. The following explanation of this form is based on the style recommended by the American Chemical Society.

### *References in the Text*
For in-text citations, you may use one of two formats: superscript numbers or reference numbers within parentheses.

The purple color of plakinidine A and B varies according to the pH[12] and is reminiscent of hue fluctuations observed for unique polycyclic aromatic alkaloids from sponges,[13,14] tunicates,[15,16] and an anemone[17].

Chemical studies (8-11) indicate that the mechanism leading to the production of high energy ions is not yet finally clear. It is known, however, that high energy ion yields are affected much less by oxygen than low energy ion yields (12).

### *List of References*

In the list of references, labelled "References," entries are arranged in order of in-text citation, not alphabetically. Titles of journal articles are not listed, titles of journals are abbreviated, and titles of both journals and books are in italics or underlined. Dates of journals are in boldface, and the volume numbers of journals are underlined or italicized.

References

(1)   Schmitz, F. J.; Agarwal, S. K.; Gunasekera, S. P.; Schmidt, P. G.; Shoolery, J. N. *J. Am. Chem. Soc.* **1983**, *105*, 4835.

(2)   Huheey, J. E. *Inorganic Chemistry: Principles of Structure and Reactivity*, 2nd ed.; Harper and Row: New York, 1978; pp 342-348.

(3)   (a) Kessler, H.; Gerke, M.; Griesinger, C. *Angew. Chem. Int. Ed. Engl.* **1988**, *27*, 490. (b) Schoolery, J. N. *J. Nat. Prod.* **1984**, *47*, 226.

Note that the in-text citation for the preceeding entry may refer either to (3), (3a), or (3b).

(4)   Honig, R. E. *J. Appl. Phys.* **1958**, *29*, 549.

(5)    Jackman, L. M. In <u>Physical Methods in Organic Chemistry</u>; Schwarz, J. C. P., Ed.; Holden-Day, Inc: San Francisco, 1964; Chapter 5.

Use the <u>Journal of the American Chemical Society</u> as a model for other kinds of references, or consult a recent style manual published by the American Chemical Society.

### Classical Studies

Students should become familiar with the use of <u>L'Annee philologique</u> (<u>Aph</u>). This valuable publications index will help you research your essay, and it will also serve as a style guide to ancient and modern spellings and abbreviations. Consult <u>The Oxford Classical Dictionary</u>, second edition (1970), edited by N. G. L. Hammond and H. H. Scullard, and <u>The Cambridge Ancient History</u>, second edition (1982), edited by J. B. Bury et al. to acquaint yourself with spellings, abbreviations, and to obtain a general orientation to the subjects covered. Examine classical studies monographs and periodicals to become familiar with common practice in matters of style. Generally, the footnoting/bibliography method is recommended; however, parenthetical documentation Style A is sometimes advised, as is Style B. Follow any guides that accompany your course syllabus. No matter what style you decide to use, use it consistently throughout your essay.

### Comparative Development Studies

In comparative development studies, as in other interdisciplinary studies, students should consult their instructor or use the form of documentation preferred in the discipline that most informs the essay being written. In a comparative development studies paper investigating economic theory or policy, for example, the form of Style B described under the heading "Economics" could be used. Likewise, the appropriate variations of Style B could be used in papers informed by political or anthropological research. If your essay focusses on comparative literature or history, on the other hand, Style A or the footnoting/bibliography method might be best. Most frequently, however, some varation of Style B will be acceptable because economics, political science, and anthropology are the disciplines upon which comparative development studies is based.

## Computer Studies

Computer science journals generally use either a form of Style B or of the number-reference method.

### *References in the Text: Style B*

The journal <u>Computational Intelligence: An International Journal</u> suggests the use of a form of Style B. References are cited in parentheses within the text by authors' last names and years of publication:

```
Many studies (Hammond and Simons 1987; Bradley 1989;
Butler 1992) indicate that the results of Butler
(1985) are valid and relevant.
```

### *List of References: Style B*

The list of references appears at the end of the paper and is labelled "References."

References

BRADLEY, J. 1989. Research challenges in information technology: hypermedia. Canadian humanities computing, 3: 4-8.

BUTLER, C. 1985. Computers in linguistics. Blackwell.

-----------1992. Computers and written texts. Blackwell.

HAMMOND, J. and C. SIMONS. 1987. The cognate language teacher: a teaching package for higher education. <u>In</u> The use of computers in the teaching of language and languages, <u>Edited by</u> G. Chesters and N. Gardner. CTISS Publications, pp. 100-107.

### References in the Text: Number-Reference Method

When following the number-reference method, use superscript numerals for in-text citations:

Many studies[1-3] indicate that the results of Butler[4] are valid and relevant.

### List of References: Number-Reference Method

Arrange and number entries in the list of references, which is usually labelled "Works Cited," according to their first mention in the paper. Journal titles may be abbreviated. Note that, for books, the publisher is listed before the place of publication.

### Works Cited

1. Nelson, T. "On the Xandu project." Byte 15 (Sept. 1990), 298-99.

2. Bradley, J. "Research challenges in information technology: hypermedia." Canadian Humanities Computing 3 (1) (Feb. 1989), 4-8.

3. Butler, C. Computers and Written Texts, Blackwell, Oxford, 1992.

4. Butler, C. Computers in Linguistics, Blackwell, Oxford, 1985.

## Cultural Studies

In interdisciplinary studies such as cultural studies, it is best to follow the documentation method preferred in the discipline which most informs your essay. In a cultural studies essay focussing on historical material, for example, the footnoting/bibliography method would be appropriate. In a cultural studies paper addressing sociological questions, however, the form of Style B used in sociological journals might be preferable.

## Economics

Economics uses a form of Style B modified in the following ways.

### References in the Text

1. The abbreviation "p." is eliminated in citations in the text: (Smith 1776, 740).

2. An "and" rather than an ampersand (&) is used when referring to sources with two authors: (Arrow and Kurz 1970).

3. When citing more than two works by the same author(s) published in the same year, only list the distinguishing lower case letter after the comma(s): (MacDonald 1988a,b).

In articles published in economics journals, authors' names seem to appear more frequently in the text than in parenthetical citations. Here is an example:

Using this rate as a social discount rate is recommended in several studies, including Marglin (1963), Feldstein (1964a), Diamond (1968), Kay (1972), Ahsan (1980), and Mendelsohn (1981, 1983).

### List of References

1. The first names of authors are usually spelled out in full in the list of references, entitled "References." Give authors' names as they appear on the title page of the source.

2. The names of second and subsequent authors appear in natural order.

3. There is no period after the date of publication, which is placed in parentheses.

4. There are quotation marks around the titles of articles in journals and books as well as around the titles of unpublished sources, including dissertations and reports, and of chapters or portions of published sources.

5. No period follows the title of a book, which is underlined or italicized.

6. The place of publication and the publisher are placed in parentheses.

7. No period closes an entry.

Here are some sample entries in the list of references:

## References

Arrow, Kenneth J., and Mordecai Kurz (1970) <u>Public Investment, the Rate of Return, and Optimal Fiscal Policy</u> (Baltimore: Johns Hopkins Press)

Demougin, Dominique, and Aloysius Siow (1991) "Careers in ongoing hierarchies." Unpublished manuscript, University of Toronto

Diamond, Peter (1973) "Taxation and public production in a growth setting." In <u>Models of Economic Growth</u>, ed. James A. Mirrlees and N. H. Stern (New York: Halsted Press)

MacDonald, Glenn (1982) "A market equilibrium theory of job assignment and sequential accumulation of information." <u>American Economic Review</u> 72, 1038-55

-- (1988a) "Job mobility in market equilibrium." <u>Review of Economic Studies</u> 55, 153-68

-- (1988b) "The economics of rising stars." <u>American Economic Review</u> 78, 155-66

Marx, Karl (1857/8) <u>The Grundrisse</u>. Text references to R. C. Tucker (1978) <u>The Marx-Engels Reader</u>, 2nd ed. (New York: W.W. Norton)

Students may refer to the <u>Canadian Journal of Economics</u> for further examples.

## Education
Most frequently, journals in this field require authors to follow the APA form of documentation, which we call Style B. See pages 97-112 for a detailed description of this style, which is based on information from the <u>Publication Manual of the American Psychological Association</u> (1983). Use the APA manual to supplement the information given in this text.

## English Literature
Students of English literature may use either the footnoting/bibliography method or parenthetical documentation Style A. If the essay focuses on only one text, or on a few texts, Style A is preferable. If, however, the essay relies on a diverse number of sources (particularly secondary sources), the footnoting/bibliography method may better provide information for the reader.

## Environmental and Resource Studies
Environmental science journals usually recommend a form of Style B. The following description of this form is based upon that required by the Canadian Journal of Fisheries and Aquatic Sciences.

### *References in the Text*
1. Do not separate the names(s) of the author(s) from the date of publication with a comma in parenthetical citations: (Walker 1980)

2. References to particular sections or pages of an item are rare in biology or environmental science papers; however, if this information is required, it should be put inside the parenthetical citation in the following way: (Walker 1980, p. 14) or (Jones 1990, fig. 3)

3. When referring to an item that has more than two authors, include only the surname of the first author followed by "et al." in either the parenthetical citation or the text of your paper: (Taylor et al. 1991) or Taylor et al. (1991) compared . . .

### *List of References*
1. In the list of references, called "References," all the letters in the authors' names are capitalized.

2. When listing a work with multiple authors in the "References" section, put the surname of the first author first and follow this with his or her initials, but place the surname of each subsequent author after her or his initials: PARSONS, T. R., Y. MARTOR, AND C. N. LORLI.

3. Journal titles are usually abbreviated according to the Serial Sources for the BIOSIS Data Base.

## References

ADDICOTT, J. F. 1978. Niche relationships among species of aphids feeding on fireweed. Can. J. Zool. 56: 1837-1851.

LEVINE, L. 1973. Biology of the gene. C. V. Mosby Co., Saint Louis.

ROSS, A. F. 1966. Systematic effects of local lesion formation, p. 127-150. In H. B. R. Beemster and J. Dijkstra [ed.] Viruses of plants. North-Holland Publ. Co., Amsterdam.

## Geography

Because this discipline deals with the earth and its life, it can be considered a social or a physical science; there are economic geographers, historical geographers, geologists, and geophysicists. Consequently, many different documentation methods are acceptable in geography. When deciding which of the four methods to use, consider your instructor's background and the journals he or she refers to most often. Frequently, geography journals use a form of parenthetical documentation similar to Style B. One variation of Style B, modelled following, is based on the method of documentation required by The Canadian Geographer, a publication of the Canadian Association of Geographers that publishes articles of interest to both physical and social geographers.

### *References in the Text*

1. The year is not separated from the author's last name by a comma, and the abbreviation "p." is not used: (Bourne 1982, 43).

2. In references to works with two authors, an "and" is used rather than an ampersand: (Brown and Brown 1983, 111).

### *List of References*

1. The list of references, entitled "References," contains only those works cited in the paper, and it should be begun on a separate page following the text.

2. The list of references is arranged in alphabetical order according to the authors' surnames. Multiple entries for a single author are arranged chronologically, by date of publication. If two or more publications by the same author(s) have the same publication date, add the suffixes a, b, c, etc. to differentiate entries.

3. The authors' names are in capital letters.

4. There are no parentheses around the date of publication.

5. The titles of articles and portions of books are in quotation marks.

6. The place of publication and publisher are enclosed in parentheses.

7. No periods separate elements of an entry.

## References

BRITTON, J.N.H. 1974 "Environmental adaptation of industrial plants: Service linkages, locational environment and organization" in <u>Spatial Perspectives on Industrial Organization and Decision Making</u>, ed F.E.I. Hamilton (Chichester, Sussex: Wiley) 363-90

HAGGETT, P. 1979 <u>Geography: A Modern Synthesis</u> (New York: Harper and Row)

LAWRENCE, E.N. 1965 "Terrestrial climate and the solar cycle" <u>Weather</u> 20, 334-43.

## History
History uses the footnoting/bibliography method.

## Interdisciplinary Studies
In interdisciplinary studies, it is important to consult your instructor about which style of documentation to use. If this is not possible, it is best to follow the documentation method preferred in the discipline which most informs the essay you are writing.

## Mathematics

The form of documentation used in mathematics varies from journal to journal, but it generally follows the number-reference method. Following is a description of the number-reference method recommended by the American Mathematical Society.

### *References in the Text*

In-text citations should be in square brackets and in boldface:

```
Facially symmetric spaces were introduced [12] and
studied in [15]. The results obtained here and in
[1], [2], and [5] are consistent.
```

### *List of References*

Entries in the list of references, entitled "References," are alphabetized and then numbered:

### References

1. H. Arnki, <u>On a characterization of the state of quantum mechanics</u>, Commun. Math. Phys. **75** (1980), 1-24.

2. Y. Friedman and B. Russo, <u>Affine structure of facially symmetric spaces</u>, Math. Proc. Camb. Philos. Soc. **106** (1981), 107-124.

3. --------, <u>Some affine geometric aspects of operator algebras</u>, Pac. J. Math. **137** (1989), 123-144.

4. H. Hanche-Alsen and E. Stormer, <u>Jordon operator algebras</u>, Pitman, London, 1984.

Note that <u>The Canadian Journal of Mathematics</u> uses the form described above except that in-text reference numbers and brackets are in regular typeface rather than in boldface.

For further information, consult your instructor or the most recent style manual published by the American Mathematical Society. Alternatively, follow the format used in <u>The Canadian Journal of Mathematics</u> or in a recent publication of the Canadian Mathematical Society or the American Mathematical Society.

## Modern Languages

Any one of the styles of documentation described in this text, as long as it is used correctly and consistently, is acceptable in modern languages. Parenthetical documentation Style A may be preferable for literature essays that focus on one or a few texts; for essays that have a diverse and large number of secondary sources, the footnoting/bibliography method may be better. The anthropological form of Style B may be most appropriate for linguistics papers.

## Native Studies

In Native studies both the footnoting/bibliography method and the parenthetical documentation method (Style A or a variation of Style B) are acceptable. Usually, journals in this discipline use a variation of Style B that is similar to that used in anthropology or archaeology journals. This variation, modelled in the Canadian Journal of Native Studies, is outlined here.

### References in the Text

1. A colon is used in place of "p." when a page reference is given: (Badgley, 1980:23).

2. When citing a source with two authors, an "and" rather than an ampersand (&) is used: (Honigmann and Honigmann, 1953:57).

3. If the names of the authors appear in the text do not repeat them in the parenthetical citations:

This is clear particularly in Powers (1977, 1982, 1986a, and 1986b).

Also do not repeat the publication date of a source if this information appears in the text of your paper:

As DeMaille and Lavenda wrote in 1977, "The concept cf power is a key to understanding the cultural systems of the Siouan peoples of the Plains" (153).

4. Cite the sources from which you took ideas and information:

Twenty eight percent of Native inmates were incarcerated for violent offenses in 1982 as compared to 7.3% of the non-Native population (LaPrairie, 1984b).

## *List of References*

### References

Badgley, R.F.
>1980   Social Policy and Indian Health Services in Canada. _Anthropological Quarterly_ 46: 150-159.

Barbeau, Marius
>1960   Huron-Wyandot Traditional Narratives. _National Museum of Canada Bulletin_ 165.

Canada. Department of Indian Affairs and Northern Development
>1980   _Indian Conditions: A Survey_. Ottawa: Department of Indian Affairs and Northern Development.

DeMaille, Raymond J. and Robert H. Lavenda
>1977   Wakan: Plains Siouan Concepts of Power, pp.153-165 in Raymond D. Fogelson and Richard N. Adams (Editors): _The Anthropology of Power: Ethnographic Studies from Asia, Oceania, and the New World_. New York: Academic Press.

LaPrairie, C.P.
>1984a  Select Socio-Economic and Criminal Justice Data on Native Women. _Canadian Journal of Criminology_ 26:161-169.
>1984b  Native Women and Crime. _Perceptions_ 7(4):25-27.

Nelms, Joyce E.
  1973    The Indian Women and Household Structure in
          Mill Creek, British Columbia. M.A. thesis,
          Department of Anthropology, University of
          Victoria. Unpublished.

Tiller, Veronica E.
  1983    Jicarilla Apache, pp. 440-461 in Alphonson
          Ortiz (Editor): Handbook of North American
          Indians. Volume 10: Southwest. Washington:
          Smithsonian Institute.

## Philosophy

Students of philosophy may use either the footnoting/bibliography method
or parenthetical documentation Style A. If the essay focuses on only one
primary text, or on a few texts, Style A is preferable. If, however, the essay
relies on a diverse number of sources (particularly secondary sources), the
footnoting/bibliography method may better provide information for the
reader.

## Physics

The American Institute of Physics recommends the following form of the
number-reference method of documentation.

### *References in the Text: American Institute of Physics*

In the paper, use superscript numerals that correspond to the numbered
entries in the list of references:

Some studied the physcical aspects of Milne's
theory.[20-26] Others raised issues regarding the
philosophical aspects of Milne's work.[5,32,40-44]

### *List of References: American Institute of Physics*

Entries in the list of references, called "References," are arranged in order
of in-text citation. Note that the volume numbers of journals are in
boldface, journal titles are abbreviated, and the titles of journal articles are
not needed. For books, underline titles, and provide specific page
references.

### References

1. R. Zallen and M. L. Slade, Phys. Rev. B. **18**, 5775 (1978).

2. A. D. Lowitz, J. Chem. Phys. **46**, 4698 (1967).

3. J. M. Jauch and F. Rohrlich, The Theory of Photons and Electrons (Springer Verlag, Berlin, 1976), pp. 457-460.

4. P. G. Burke and K. Smith, Can. J. Phys. **49**, 2875-2885 (1971).

5. W. Siegel, Phys. Lett. **94B**, 37 (1980); L. V. Audeev and O. V. Tarasov, Phys. Lett. **112B**, 356 (1982); L. V. Audeev and A. A. Vladimirov, Nucl. Phys. **B219**, 262 (1983).

### *References in Text: Canadian Journal of Physics*
The Canadian Journal of Physics requires a slightly different form of the number-reference method. The in-text reference numbers are in parentheses, like this (6, 7) or (20).

### *List of References: Canadian Journal of Physics*
References in the list of references look like this:

### References

1. V. ELIAS, G. MCKEON, and R. B. MANN. Can. J. Phys. **63**, 1498 (1985).

2. A. R. SINGH. In Physico-chemical processes. Vol. 2. Edited by G. Ball. Academic Press, New York. 1982. pp. 18-22.

3. L. ROBIN. In Proceedings of the 4th International Conference on Kinetics, London, June 4-5, 1980. Edited by J. Jones. Plenum Press, London. 1981. pp. 98-103.

4. E. PRUGOVECKI. Quantum mechanics in Hilbert space. Academic Press Inc., New York. 1981.

Use either the <u>Canadian Journal of Physics</u> or the most recent style manual published by the American Institute of Physics to find more information on and models of the two formats described here.

## Political Science

Although both parenthetical documentation and the footnoting/bibliography method are acceptable in political science, the footnoting/bibliography method is recommended by most journals in the discipline, including the <u>Canadian Journal of Political Science</u>.

## Psychology

Psychology uses Style B. See pages 97-112 for a detailed description of this style, which is based on information from the <u>Publication Manual of the American Psychological Association</u> (1983). Use this manual for other kinds of references.

## Sociology

Sociology uses a form of Style B. Students should make the following changes to that style.

### *References in the Text*

1. Separate the date of publication and the location reference with a colon: (Hochschild, 1989: 15-17) or (Smith, 1989: Figure 2.3)

### *List of References*

1. In the list of references, entitled "References," the titles of books and journals are underlined, and the titles of chapters in books, articles in books, and articles in periodicals are placed in quotation marks.

2. If there are two or more authors, list the second and subsequent authors with their first names first and their surnames last in the "References" section.

Pay close attention to the spacing, layout, and punctuation of the following examples.

## References

Bellamy, Leslie and Neil Guppy
1991 "Opportunities and obstacles for women in Canadian higher education." In J. Gaskell and A. McLaren, eds., Women and Education, 2nd edition, pp. 163-92. Calgary: Detselig.

Boyd, Monica, John Goyder, Frank E. Jones, Hugh A. McRoberts, Peter Pineo, and John Porter
1985 Ascription and Achievement: Studies in Mobility and Status Attainment in Canada. Ottawa: Carleton University Press.

Gabin, Nancy Felice
1984 Women Auto Workers and the United Automobile Workers' Union (UAW-CIO), 1935-1955. Unpublished Ph.D. Dissertation. University of Michigan.

Koch, Dorothea
1990 Interview, July 26.

Lenski, Gerhard
1991 "Positivism's future — and sociology's." Canadian Journal of Sociology 16(2):187-95.

Psacharopoulos, George, ed.
1987 Economics of Education: Research and Studies. New York: Pergamon Press.

Turner, Jonathan H.
1975a "A strategy for reformulating the dialectical and functional conflict theories." Social Forces 53(2): 433-44.
1975b "Marx and Simmel revisited." Social Forces 53(3): 619-27.

## Statistics

Statistical journals usually recommend either a variation of Style B or the number-reference method of documentation. Check with your instructor to discover the method he or she prefers. If this is not possible, follow the method recommended by the American Mathematical Society and outlined under the heading "Mathematics" in this list.

## Women's Studies

In interdisciplinary studies such as women's studies, it is best to follow the documentation method preferred in the discipline which most informs the essay being written. For example, in a women's studies essay focussing on historical material, the footnoting/bibliography method would be appropriate; in a women's studies paper addressing sociological questions, the form of Style B used in sociological journals would be best.

# PART VI:
## —— LIST OF RECOMMENDED BOOKS ——

A small book like <u>Notes</u> cannot cover all the intricacies of documentation and essay writing. The texts listed below will provide more detailed information on various aspects of essay preparation.

### Documentation and Format

<u>The Chicago Manual of Style</u>. 13th ed. Chicago: U of Chicago P, 1982.

Council of Biology Editors, Committee on Form and Style. <u>CBE Style Manual</u>. 5th ed. Bethesda, MD: Council of Biology Editors, 1983.

Gibaldi, Joseph, and Walter S. Achtert. <u>MLA Handbook for Writers of Research Papers</u>. 3rd ed. New York: The Modern Language Association of America, 1988.

American Psychological Association. <u>Publication Manual of the American Psychological Association</u>. 3rd ed. Washington, DC: American Psychological Association, 1983.

Turabian, Kate L. <u>A Manual for Writers of Term Papers, Theses, and Dissertations</u>. 5th ed. Chicago: U of Chicago P, 1987.

### Essay Preparation—General

Avery, Heather, et al. <u>Thinking It Through: A Practical Guide to Academic Essay Writing</u>. 2nd ed. Peterborough, ON: Academic Skills Centre, Trent U, 1989.

Barzun, Jacques, and Henry Graff. <u>The Modern Researcher: The Classic Manual on All Aspects of Research and Writing</u>. 4th ed. New York: Harcourt Brace Jovanovitch, 1985.

Flower, Linda. <u>Problem-Solving Strategies for Writing</u>. 3rd ed. Toronto: Harcourt Brace Jovanovich, 1989.

Giltrow, Janet. <u>Academic Writing: How to Read and Write Scholarly Prose</u>. Peterborough, ON: Broadview P, 1990.

### Essay Preparation—Discipline-Specific

Barnet, Sylvan. <u>A Short Guide to Writing about Literature</u>. 5th ed. Toronto: Scott Foresman, 1985.

Benjamin, Jules R. <u>A Student's Guide to History</u>. 5th ed. New York: St. Martin's, 1991.

Friedman, Sharon, and Stephen Steinberg. <u>Writing and Thinking in the Social Sciences</u>. Englewood Cliffs, NJ: Prentice-Hall, 1989.

Keene, Michael. <u>Effective Professional Writing</u>. Toronto: D.C. Heath, 1987.

Martinich, A.P. <u>Philosophical Writing: An Introduction</u>. Englewood Cliffs, NJ: Prentice-Hall, 1989.

### Grammar, Style, and Usage

Barzun, Jacques. <u>Simple and Direct: A Rhetoric for Writers</u>. Rev. ed. New York: HarperCollins, 1985.

Boyne, Martin and Don LePan. <u>Common Errors in English: An ESL Guide</u>. Peterborough, ON: Broadview P, 1993

Coe, Richard. <u>Process, Form, and Substance: A Rhetoric for Advanced Writers</u>. 2nd ed. Englewood Cliffs, NJ: Prentice-Hall, 1990.

LePan, Don. <u>The Broadview Book of Common Errors in English</u>. 2nd ed. Peterborough, ON: Broadview P, 1992.

Messenger, William, and Jan de Bruyn. <u>The Canadian Writer's Handbook</u>. 2nd ed. Scarborough, ON: Prentice-Hall, 1986.

Moore, Michael D. <u>A Writer's Handbook of Current English</u>. 3rd Canadian ed. Toronto: Gage, 1988.

Strunk, William Jr., and E.B. White. <u>The Elements of Style</u>. 3rd ed. New York: Macmillan, 1979.

Taylor, Karen, et al. <u>Clear, Correct, Creative: A Handbook for Writers of Academic Prose</u>. Peterborough, ON: Academic Skills Centre, Trent U, 1991.

Thomson, A.J., and A.V. Martinet. <u>A Practical English Grammar</u>. 3rd ed. Oxford: Oxford UP, 1980.

### Studying

Fleet, Joan, Fiona Goodchild, and Richard Zajchowski. <u>Learning for Success: Skills and Strategies for Canadian Students</u>. Toronto: Harcourt Brace Jovanovich, 1990.

Pauk, Walter. <u>How to Study in College</u>. 4th ed. Boston: Houghton Mifflin, 1989.

Taylor, Catherine, et al. <u>Making Your Mark: Learning to Do Well on Exams</u>. Peterborough, ON: Academic Skills Centre, Trent U, 1988.

## Graphic Illustration

Tufte, Edward R. <u>The Visual Display of Quantitative Information</u>. Cheshire, CT: Graphics P, 1983.

# Index

Abbreviations **14-16**, 23, 25, 70
  *anon.*, use of 54, 84
  *cf*, use of 71
  *chap.*, use of 98
  *diss.*, use of 62, 91
  *ed.*, use of 52, 54, 57, 82, 84, 104, 105
  *et al.*, use of 23, 53, 76, 83, 99, 100, 119, 123, 133
  *Fig.*, use of 28, 98
  *ibid.*, use of 70
  *illus.*, use of 28
  in anthropology/archaeology 119
  in biology 124
  in bibliographies 88, 95
  in chemistry 127
  in classical studies 128
  in computer studies 130
  in economics 131
  in environmental and resource studies 133
  in footnotes 51, 57, 58, 60, 63, 67, 69, 70
  in geography 134
  in list of references (Style A) 88, 95
  in list of references (Style B) 104, 105, 106, 107
  in parenthetical references (Style A) 72, 77,
  in parenthetical references (Style B) 98
  in physics 139
  *loc. cit.*, use of 70
  *M.A.*, use of 91
  *n. pag.*, use of 63
  *n.d.*, use of 63, 91
  *n.p.*, use of 63, 91
  *N.p.*, use of 63, 91
  of foreign words 23
  of journal titles 124, 127, 130, 133, 139
  of provinces and territories 15
  of states 15, 16
  of units of measurement 23, 25
  *op. cit.*, use of 70
  *p.* and *pp.*, use of 98, 106, 107
  *prod.*, use of 66, 94, 95
  *qtd.*, use of 68, 77
  *sic*, use of 37
Abstracts
  in list of references (Style B) 109
  use of in research 5

Acronyms  *See* Abbreviations
Actors, reference to
  in footnotes 66
  in list of references (Style A) 94
Acts of plays
  in footnotes 56, 58, 68-69
  in parenthetical references (Style A) 77
Addresses (Speeches)
  in bibliographies 93
  in footnotes 64
  in list of references (Style A) 93
Adjectives, capitalization of 18, 19
Administrative studies
  documentation method used in 119
Afterwords
  in bibliographies 86
  in footnotes 58
  in list of references (Style A) 86
Alphabetization
  in bibliographies 79, 84
  in list of references (Style A) 79, 84
  in list of references (Style B) 103
  in parenthetical references (Style B) 102
  in the number-reference method 113, 115-116, 118
American Mathematical Society
  documentation method recommended by 136, 143
American Psychological Association (APA) 47, 97
  method of documentation recommended by *See* APA style
Ampersand, use of in parenthetical references (Style B) 99
Analysis **8-9**, 32, 39
*anon.*, 54, 84
Anonymous works
  in bibliographies 84, 87, 89, 91
  in footnotes 54, 58, 60, 63
  in list of references (Style A) 84, 87, 89, 91
  in list of references (Style B) 104, 108
  in parenthetical references (Style B) 101
Anthologies
  in bibliographies 86
  in footnotes 57- 58
  in list of references (Style A) 86
Anthropology
  documentation method used in 119-122

To order copies of *Notes on the Preparation of Essays in the Arts and Sciences* and other Academic Skills Centre publications found in the list of recommended books, contact the Academic Skills Centre by mail, telephone, or facsimile:

Academic Skills Centre
Trent University
Peterborough, Ontario
Canada   K9J 7B8

Telephone: (705) 748-1720     Facsimile: (705) 748-1721

Bulk orders of ten or more copies are sold at a 20% reduction in price.